Betty Crocker's
Slow Cooker
COOKBOOK

WILEY

Wiley Publishing, Inc.

Library of Congress Cataloging-in-Publication Data

Crocker, Betty.
  [Slow cooker cookbook]
  Betty Crocker's slow cooker cookbook.
    p. cm.
  ISBN 0-02-863469-1
  1. Electric cookery, Slow. I. Title II. Title: Slow cooker cookbook.
  TX827.C75 1999   99-35736
  641.5'884—dc21   CIP

General Mills, Inc.

Betty Crocker Kitchens
Manager, Publishing: Lois L. Tlusty
Editor: Lois L. Tlusty
Recipe Development: Altanette Autry, Phyllis Kral
Food Stylists: Mary Johnson, Cindy Ojczyk, Carol Grones
Nutritionists: Nancy Holmes, R.D.
Photographic Services:
Art Director: Pam Kurtz
Photographer: Nanci Doonan Dixon

Cover and Book design by Michele Laseau

For consistent baking results, the Betty Crocker Kitchens recommend Gold Medal Flour

Manufactured in the China
15 14 13 12 11 10
First Edition

Cover photo: Beef Stew with Sun-Dried Tomatoes (page 42)

Greetings—

Do you want dinner ready and waiting? Well, you've come to the right place. With your slow cooker and these easy flavor-packed recipes, you can get a jump start on dinner in the morning without much effort . Plus, you come home to the enticing aroma of a home-cooked meal. Best of all, you can relax—dinner just about makes itself!

Your slow cooker is not only for the work-a-day world but also for carefree entertaining. Slow cookers are ideal for serving a hot beverage, warm dip or on the buffet table because it keeps food hot and tasty for several hours. Look for this crowd-size symbol: next to recipes to serve the next time family and friends gather at your home.

Crowd
SIZE

Your slow cooker is the perfect partner when you're on the go, too. Whether it's a scout's banquet, a party at work or a neighbor's potluck—you'll have no problem packing up your dish and keeping it hot.

So get ready to discover all the tasty simmered-in flavors of slow cooking.

Betty Crocker

P.S. I love my slow cooker!

Conte

n t s

Joy of Slow Cooking

Slow and Steady Cooking

In today's busy world, things just seem to be getting faster, including the time we spend preparing meals. What a surprise to discover that using a slow cooker is an answer to everyday dinner. Slow cooking is the best way to keep pace with our busy lives since the meal you're making requires little to no attention while it cooks, and you'll enjoy a home-cooked, good-for-you meal.

Designed for economy and ease as well as for comfort and convenience, this slow, steady cooking method fits into every life-style. Put the ingredients into the slow cooker, then cover and let it cook while you are at work, running errands, or enjoying the day outside. Small families and individuals can also enjoy the benefits of slow cooking, since you can make enough to enjoy "planned-overs" on another day. And nothing is quite as welcoming as coming home to the rich aroma of a home-cooked meal wafting through the house. Invest in the convenience and comfort of slow cooking. It offers a variety of advantages.

Energy Efficient

Slow cooking uses very little electricity because the wattage used is low. Consumers benefit because this is a low-cost way to prepare a meal.

Cool Cooking

Slow cooking isn't just for stews and soups during the winter. You can do it all year round, and without using the oven during the summer, the kitchen stays cooler. It's also great when your oven is in use and you want to make side dishes or desserts.

Perfectly Portable

A slow cooker is the perfect appliance for motor homes, to take to the cabin and for college students. It eliminates the need for multiple pots and pans. It is great to carry along to potlucks, parties and other social events because your dish will stay warm.

No Clock Watching

If you are stuck in traffic or running late for an appointment, not to worry! An extra half or full hour on the low setting will not ruin a meal in the slow cooker.

Easy Preparation

Cut vegetables and meat when you have the time (you can even brown the meat ahead of time!), wrap them separately and refrigerate, then place them in the slow cooker the next morning. Dinner will be ready and waiting when you get home, and even you will be surprised by how easy it was!

Moist and Flavorful

Slow cooking allows the juices of foods to blend and create tender, flavorful dishes, and the meat generally shrinks less.

Make and Take

Office party or meeting with the troops? Wrap the slow cooker in a towel or newspaper to insulate it, and place it in a box that will stay flat in your car. Serve the food within an hour, or plug in the cooker and set it on the low heat setting so it will stay warm for hours.

Meals in Minutes

Slow-cooker meals cook themselves. When you add bread, a salad or a vegetable, and a beverage, the meal is ready to set on the table in minutes.

Slow-Cooking Savvy

Although using a slow cooker is pretty simple, boning up on the basics is a good idea so you'll be familiar with what slow cookers offer. Here's a brief rundown of the two types of slow cookers available, both designed to ensure even cooking with an automatic control.

Continuous Slow Cooker

The food cooks continuously at a very low wattage. The heating coils are in the outer metal shell. The coils become hot and stay on constantly to heat the crockery liner. This type of cooker has two or three fixed settings: low (about 200°), high (about 300°) and in some newer models, auto, which shifts from high to low automatically. The ceramic liner may be fixed or removable. Removable liners offer easy cleanup.

Intermittent Crockery Cooker

This cooker has a heating element in the base on which the cooking container stands. The heat cycles on and off (like an oven) to maintain a constant temperature. The cookers have a dial with numbers or temperatures. Be sure to follow the use-and-care book that comes with the cooker to determine what settings to use. Often, the lowest setting/temperature is only for keeping foods warm, not for cooking.

Slow cookers range in size from a 1- to 6-quart capacity. The 1-quart size is perfect for making and keeping dips and spreads warm for a party. The larger sizes are ideal for cooking one-dish meals and other family favorites. We have included a range of appropriate size cookers at the top of each recipe.

High or Low?

Most slow cookers have low and high control settings. At the low heat setting, the food temperature remains just below the boiling point. Many recipes use the low heat setting because the longer cooking time often fits better into your daily schedule. You can start dinner before leaving your home in the morning, and it is ready when you return.

At the high heat setting, liquid gently bubbles and cooks approximately twice as fast as on low heat. It is always best to use the heat setting that a recipe recommends, but sometimes you prefer a shorter cook time. Use the guide that 1 hour on high is equal to 2 to 2 1/2 hours of cooking on low. So if you don't have 8 to 10 hours for dinner to cook on the low heat setting, use high instead, and it should be ready to eat in 4 to 5 hours.

After the food is cooked, it can be held at the low heat setting up to an hour or so without overcooking. Remember, it is best to check occasionally to see whether it needs to be stirred.

A Watched Crock Never Cooks...

A slow cooker that's opened doesn't cook, so don't peek! Keep the cover on unless a recipe tells you to remove it. Removing the cover allows heat to escape and adds 15 to 20 minutes to the cooking time each time you peek.

How Full?

For best results, a slow cooker should be between one-half and three-fourths full of food. This helps to ensure that the liquid will not cook away during the long hours of cooking. It also helps keep the food moist and tender.

Finishing Cook Time

You'll see that some recipes have a "Finishing Cook Time" included. This is necessary when a slow cooker recipe isn't completely "self-sufficient" and a few minutes of additional cooking is required. It can be making fluffy dumplings on a hearty beef stew, adding pasta to soup or to thicken the juices to make a richer tasting sauce. We've brought this to your attention to let you know that someone will have to be around for those additional 15 to 30 minutes of cooking.

Oops! The Power's Out

What should you do if the power goes off and you aren't at home while your slow cooker is in use? It is best not to eat the food even if it looks done. If the power has been turned off for a length of time, the food may have stood at too low a temperature to be safe.

However, if you are home, you can put the uncooked food in another pan and finish cooking it on the stove, if it is gas, or on an outdoor grill. Or store it in a cooler with ice if the power might be off for some time and you have no way to continue cooking.

If you are home while using your slow cooker and you know the food is completely cooked, it can safely stay in the cooker up to 2 hours with the power off. Don't lift the lid so that the temperature won't drop.

Storing and Serving Leftovers

Be sure to remove any remaining food from the slow cooker within 1 hour after it is finished cooking and store it in the refrigerator. We recommend not reheating leftovers in the slow cooker because it takes too long for the food to reach a safe internal temperature. It is best to reheat leftovers in the microwave or on top of the stove.

If you made a dish ahead and stored in the refrigerator but want to serve it in the slow cooker, that is fine. Just reheat the food on top of the stove or in the microwave. Then put it in a preheated slow cooker to keep hot and to serve.

Adapt Your Favorite Recipes

One benefit of using a slow cooker is that you can adapt mom's favorite recipe for beef stew or your most-requested vegetarian chili recipe. There's no need to hunt for a new recipe! Using the following guidelines to help, you can adapt many of your favorite recipes for making in a cooker.

First, begin by finding a similar recipe in this cookbook. It will serve as a guide for quantities, amount of liquid and cooking time. Next, unless you're making a soup, decrease the amount of liquid in your recipe to about half because liquids do not boil away. For soups, simply leave liquid level as recommended.

You can make recipes that use less-expensive cuts of meat because they become very tender in the moist-heat, low-temperature slow cooker. It is a good idea to trim as much visible fat as possible from meat before cooking so there is less fat to remove from the finished dish before serving it.

If poultry isn't browned in a skillet before adding to the cooker, it is best to remove the skin first. This not only helps reduce calories, but it also improves the appearance of the cooked pieces. Always cook and drain any type of ground meat, whether it is beef, pork or poultry, before placing it in the slow cooker. The temperatures reached in a cooker may not become hot enough quickly enough to kill any bacteria that ground meats may contain.

Dense root vegetables, such as carrots, potatoes and turnips, often take longer than meat to cook when cooked together in a slow cooker. So cut them into small, bite-size pieces and place them in the bottom of the cooker. That way, the juices from the meat drip down and help the vegetables cook.

We have found that the flavor of dried basil strengthens during long cooking. If adapting a recipe using dried basil, we suggest that you cut the amount called for in half or add fresh basil during the last 30 minutes of cooking time.

Dairy products, such as milk, sour cream and cheese, break down during long cooking times, and the sauce will be curdled. Instead of using fresh milk, try canned condensed soups, nonfat dry milk powder or canned evaporated milk for a smooth, creamy sauce. For best results, add cream, sour cream or cheese during the last 30 minutes of cooking time or just before serving to prevent them from breaking down.

Finally, be sure to allow sufficient cooking time. Most soups, stews and one-dish meals require 8 to 10 hours on the low heat setting.

Secrets of the Slow Cooker

Little "secrets," or tips and tricks, often make a recipe come out just right! From a picture-perfect appearance to the fork-tender meat and delicious vegetables, these success tips help ensure each slow-cooked meal comes with a healthy dose of praise.

First Things First!

Spray the inside of the slow cooker with cooking spray for easy cleanup.

Root vegetables, such as carrots and potatoes, take longer to cook, so cut these vegetables into small pieces or thinly slice them and place in the bottom of the slow cooker for best results.

Remove the skin from poultry, and trim excess fat from meats to reduce excess fat in the finished dish and reduce calories.

Always cook and drain ground meats before adding them to the slow cooker.

Brown meats or poultry in a skillet before adding to the slow cooker. It isn't necessary, but it can enhance the flavor and appearance of the finished dish.

Thaw frozen vegetables or rinse them with warm water to separate before placing them in the slow cooker. Adding frozen vegetables will lower the internal temperature, and the dish will take longer to cook.

Full of Flavor

Use dried leaf herbs instead of ground because they keep more flavor during the long cooking time. Another way to ensure sufficient flavor is to stir in fresh herbs during the last hour of cooking. Always taste before serving to see whether additional seasoning is needed.

Concentrate the flavor of juices in the slow cooker by removing the lid and cooking on the high heat setting during the last 20 to 30 minutes.

To create a more pronounced flavor in soups and stews, substitute broth for the water or add bouillon cubes with the water.

Ground red pepper (cayenne) and red pepper sauce tend to strengthen and become bitter during long slow cooking. Use small amounts and taste during the last hour of cooking and decide whether more seasoning is needed.

Safety Check

For food-safety reasons, keep this checklist in mind as you use your slow cooker.

➤ Thaw meat and poultry in the refrigerator or in a microwave oven following the manufacturer's directions. Do not thaw at room temperature.

- Cook and drain all ground meat before adding it to the slow cooker to help destroy any bacteria that the meat may contain.

- We recommend not cooking whole poultry, such as chicken, turkey and Rock Cornish hens, in a slow cooker. It takes too long for a safe cooking temperature to reach the bone.

- Always remove leftovers from the slow cooker and refrigerate or freeze them as soon as you are finished eating. Cooked food shouldn't stand at room temperature longer than 1 hour.

- Don't undercook foods. For food-safety reasons, slow cooker recipes containing raw poultry or beef should cook a minimum of three hours.

- The temperature in the middle of the food being cooked must reach 140° within 1 1/2 hours and remain at or above 140° for at least 30 minutes at the setting used. For this reason, do not use frozen ingredients, and do not assemble recipes and refrigerate ahead of time. (But it is okay to prep the ingredients and refrigerate separately ahead of time. Just don't combine them until you are ready to cook.) Refrigerated ingredients, such as meat and poultry, can be used right from the refrigerator.

- To save time in the morning, you can peel and cut up vegetables the night before. Put the vegetables and meat in separate containers, cover and refrigerate. They are ready to pop into the cooker in the morning.

Cooking Meats in Your Slow Cooker

Meats prepared in a slow cooker do not brown like they do when cooked in a skillet or an oven.

Browning meats before placing them in the slow cooker isn't necessary, but browning in a skillet or under the broiler does help eliminate excess fat and produce the flavor that some people prefer.

For meats to cook evenly, allow spaces between pieces so the heat can circulate and seasonings can be distributed.

Coating pot roasts and stew meat with flour will help to thicken the liquid as it cooks.

Before serving pot roast, meaty soups or stews, skim off excess fat with a slice of bread or skim off with a spoon.

Thickening the Juices

Because slow cookers are closed during the entire cooking period, liquids don't easily evaporate. Therefore, flavorful juices develop as the food cooks. You can use the juices without thickening, or if you prefer, thicken it to make gravy. It takes a little extra time, but it's worth the effort!

To make gravy to serve with a roast, first remove the roast from the slow cooker; cover and keep it warm. Remove the juices from the cooker and measure 1 cup for each cup of gravy. Pour the juices into a saucepan. Mix together 1 tablespoon cornstarch and 1 tablespoon cold water for each cup of liquid. Stir mixture into juices in saucepan. Cook over medium heat, stirring occasionally, until mixture boils. Boil and stir 1 to 2 minutes or until slightly thickened.

For stews or other main dishes, you will want to thicken the entire dish. Turn the cooker to high heat setting. For each 2 cups of liquid, mix 1/4 cup all-purpose flour and 1/4 cup cold water. Or if you prefer cornstarch, mix 2 tablespoons cornstarch and 2 tablespoons cold water for each 2 cups liquid. Stir mixture into the cooker. Cover and cook 20 to 30 minutes.

Beans, Beans!

Cooking dried beans in a slow cooker can be tricky because of the variations in electrical power and the types of minerals found in your local water. Beans need sufficient heat to tenderize them; dried beans cooked on the low heat setting for 8 to 10 hours may not be tender. We found three ways to cook dried beans, and you can select the one that best fits your schedule. The most convenient way to cook a dried bean recipe is to put all the ingredients into the slow cooker and cook on the high heat setting until the beans are tender. We used this method for most of the dried bean recipes.

Another method is to cook the beans 2 to 3 hours on the high heat setting, then reduce to the low heat setting for 8 to 10 hours. This is a little less convenient because you have to be available after a couple of hours to reduce the heat setting.

A more traditional method for cooking dried beans is to first place the beans and water in the slow cooker. Cover and cook on the high heat setting 2 hours. Turn off the cooker, and let beans stand 8 to 24 hours. Change the water. Add remaining ingredients, and cook on the low heat setting 8 to 12 hours or until done. We used this method for the Old-Fashioned Baked Beans recipe on page 140 because this allows the flavors to blend and offers more of an oven-baked taste.

High Altitude Tips

For people who live at higher altitudes (3,500 feet and above), everyday cooking has some challenges, and slow cooking is no exception. Unfortunately, trial and error often is the only way to make improvements because no set rules apply to all recipes.

Here are some guidelines to keep in mind when using your cooker:

Most foods will take longer to cook, particularly meats cooked in boiling liquid. Sometimes it takes twice as long than the recipe suggests for meats to become tender. You might want to try cooking meats on high heat setting rather than low to help shorten the cooking time.

Cutting vegetables into smaller pieces than suggested in the recipe will help them cook more quickly.

Dried beans also will cook more slowly. We recommend using the method of soaking them overnight in water before cooking in the slow cooker.

You can call your local U.S. Department of Agriculture (USDA) Extension Service office, listed in the phone book under county government, with questions about slow cooking at high altitude.

Simmering
One-pot
Meals

◄ *Burgundy Stew with Herb Dumplings (page 44)*

Vegetable Minestrone

■ 8 servings ■

SLOW COOKER:
3 1/2- to 6-quart

PREP TIME:
20 minutes

COOK TIME:
Low 7 to 9 hours
High 3 1/2 to 4 1/2 hours

FINISHING COOK TIME:
High 15 to 20 minutes

Ingredient Substitution

The kids will love the little corkscrew rotini pasta in this vegetable-packed soup, but elbow macaroni—that good old standby—works just as well.

Serving Suggestion

Minestrone means "big soup," and this big soup needs only thick slices of a seedy whole-grain bread to make a "big meal."

Finishing Touch

Adding the snap pea pods at the beginning with the other vegetables makes this soup easy, but if you like a brighter green, add them with the pasta at the end. Or if you don't have any pea pods, just leave them out, and your soup still will be colorful and tasty.

1 medium yellow summer squash, cut lengthwise in half, then cut crosswise into 1-inch pieces

2 medium carrots, cut into 1/4-inch slices (1 cup)

1 medium bell pepper, chopped (1 cup)

1 cup snap pea pods

1/3 cup chopped onion

4 cups water

1 jar (25 1/2 ounces) marinara sauce

1 can (15 to 16 ounces) kidney beans, rinsed and drained

1 1/2 cups uncooked rotini pasta (4 1/2 ounces)

1 teaspoon sugar

1 teaspoon salt

1/4 teaspoon pepper

Shredded Parmesan cheese, if desired

1. Mix squash, carrots, bell pepper, pea pods, onion, water, marinara sauce and beans in 3 1/2- to 6-quart slow cooker.

2. Cover and cook on low heat setting 7 to 9 hours (or high heat setting 3 1/2 to 4 1/2 hours) or until vegetables are tender.

3. Stir in pasta, sugar, salt and pepper.

4. Cover and cook on high heat setting 15 to 20 minutes or until pasta is tender. Sprinkle each serving with cheese.

1 Serving: Calories 260 (Calories from Fat 35); Fat 4g (Saturated 1g); Cholesterol 0mg; Sodium 920mg; Carbohydrate 53g (Dietary Fiber 7g); Protein 10g

% Daily Value: Vitamin A 32%; Vitamin C 30%; Calcium 6%; Iron 20%

Diet Exchanges: 3 Starch, 1 Vegetable

Creamy Leek and Potato Soup

■ 8 servings ■

SLOW COOKER:
3 1/2- to 6-quart

PREP TIME:
20 minutes

COOK TIME:
Low 8 to 10 hours
High 4 to 5 hours

FINISHING COOK TIME:
Low 20 to 30 minutes

6 medium leeks (2 pounds), thinly sliced

4 medium potatoes (1 1/2 pounds), cut into 1/2-inch cubes

2 cans (14 1/2 ounces each) ready-to-serve chicken or vegetable broth

1/4 cup margarine or butter

1/2 teaspoon salt

1/4 teaspoon pepper

1 cup half-and-half

Chopped fresh chives, if desired

1. Mix all ingredients except half-and-half and chives in 3 1/2- to 6-quart slow cooker.

2. Cover and cook on low heat setting 8 to 10 hours (or high heat setting 4 to 5 hours) or until vegetables are tender.

3. Pour vegetable mixture by batches into blender or food processor. Cover and blend on high speed until smooth; return to cooker. Stir in half-and-half.

4. Cover and cook on low heat setting 20 to 30 minutes or until hot. Sprinkle with chives.

1 Serving: Calories 190 (Calories from Fat 90); Fat 10g (Saturated 3g); Cholesterol 10mg; Sodium 720mg; Carbohydrate 22g (Dietary Fiber 3g); Protein 6g

% Daily Value: Vitamin A 12%; Vitamin C 16%; Calcium 8%; Iron 12%

Diet Exchanges: 1 Starch, 1 Vegetable, 2 Fat

Betty's Success Tip

Leeks grow best in sand soil and the broad, flat leaves of a leek wrap around each other, making the perfect place for sand to hide. The easiest way to remove the sand is to cut the leek lengthwise, almost to the root end. Hold the leek under cool running water while fanning the leaves, so the water can wash out the sand.

Ingredient Substitution

Leeks are very tasty but do take a few more minutes to clean. To save time, use a chopped large onion instead of the leeks. Or use a chopped medium onion and, for a little color, 1/2 cup sliced green onions.

Serving Suggestion

This is really an all-season soup. Serve it warm on a chilly evening, and sprinkle each serving with crumbled cooked bacon to added a hearty smoke flavor. Or in the summer, chill it in the refrigerator, and you'll have a delicious, refreshing chilled soup ready to enjoy on the deck.

French Onion Soup

■ *8 servings* ■

SLOW COOKER:
3 1/2- to 6-quart

PREP TIME:
50 minutes

STARTING COOK TIME:
High 30 to 35 minutes

COOK TIME:
Low 7 to 9 hours
High 3 to 4 hours

Betty's Success Tip

Here's some "broth math" to help you if don't have any ready-to-serve beef broth on hand. You can use three 10 1/2-ounce cans of condensed beef broth with 2 1/2 soup cans of water or 7 cups of your homemade beef broth. Or add 7 cups of water with 7 beef bouillon cubes or 2 heaping tablespoons of beef bouillon granules.

Ingredient Substitution

Vegetarians in your family? Use 4 cans of ready-to-serve vegetable broth instead of the beef broth. The color will not be a rich, deep brown, though, so Golden French Onion Soup may be a more appropriate name!

3 large onions, sliced (3 cups)

3 tablespoons margarine or butter, melted

3 tablespoons all-purpose flour

1 tablespoon Worcestershire sauce

1 teaspoon sugar

1/4 teaspoon pepper

4 cans (14 1/2 ounces each) ready-to-serve beef broth

Cheesy Broiled French Bread (below)

1. Mix onions and margarine in 3 1/2- to 6-quart slow cooker.

2. Cover and cook on high heat setting 30 to 35 minutes or until onions begin to slightly brown around edges.

3. Mix flour, Worcestershire sauce, sugar and pepper. Stir flour mixture and broth into onions. Cover and cook on low heat setting 7 to 9 hours (or high heat setting 3 to 4 hours) or until onions are very tender.

4. Prepare Cheesy Broiled French Bread. Place 1 slice bread on top of each bowl of soup. Serve immediately.

Cheesy Broiled French Bread

8 slices French bread, 1 inch thick

3/4 cup shredded mozzarella cheese (3 ounces)

2 tablespoons grated or shredded Parmesan cheese

Set oven control to broil. Place bread slices on rack in broiler pan. Sprinkle with cheeses. Broil with tops 5 to 6 inches from heat about 3 minutes or until cheese is melted.

1 Serving: Calories 185 (Calories from Fat 70); Fat 8g (Saturated 3g); Cholesterol 5mg; Sodium 1240mg; Carbohydrate 21g (Dietary Fiber 2g); Protein 9g

% Daily Value: Vitamin A 6%; Vitamin C 2%; Calcium 14%; Iron 8%

Diet Exchanges: 1 Starch, 2 Vegetable, 1 Fat

Borscht

■ 6 servings ■

SLOW COOKER:
3 1/2- to 6-quart

PREP TIME:
10 minutes

COOK TIME:
Low 6 to 8 hours
High 3 to 4 hours

2 cans (16 ounces each) diced beets, undrained

2 cans (10 1/2 ounces each) condensed beef broth

1 small onion, finely chopped (1/4 cup)

2 cups shredded cabbage

1 tablespoon sugar

1 tablespoon lemon juice

3/4 cup sour cream, if desired

Chopped fresh dill weed, if desired

1. Mix all ingredients except sour cream and dill weed in 3 1/2- to 6-quart slow cooker.

2. Cover and cook on low heat setting 6 to 8 hours (or high heat setting 3 to 4 hours) or until cabbage is tender.

3. Top each serving with sour cream and dill weed.

1 Serving: Calories 70 (Calories from Fat 10); Fat 1g (Saturated 0g); Cholesterol 0mg; Sodium 720mg; Carbohydrate 15g (Dietary Fiber 3g); Protein 3g

% Daily Value: Vitamin A 0%; Vitamin C 12%; Calcium 4%; Iron 16%

Diet Exchanges: 3 Vegetable

Betty's Success Tip

Shredding cabbage is easy when you use a long, sharp knife. Cut the cabbage into fourths, and remove the core. Thinly slice the fourths by cutting across the leaves to make long, thin strips.

Ingredient Substitution

Instead of shredding cabbage, you can use cabbage slaw mix found in the produce section of the supermarket. If other vegetables, such as shredded carrots, are in the mix, they will just add to the flavor of the soup.

Serving Suggestion

This streamlined version of the colorful eastern European favorite can be served hot or chilled. Serve it hot tonight for dinner. Any leftover soup will be ready in the refrigerator for a quick, no-fuss lunch.

Chicken and Rice Gumbo Soup

■ 6 servings ■

SLOW COOKER:
3 1/2- to 6-quart

PREP TIME:
30 minutes

COOK TIME:
Low 7 to 8 hours

FINISHING COOK TIME:
Low 20 minutes

Betty's Success Tip

Forget to put the okra in the refrigerator to thaw? No problem. To quickly thaw it, rinse under cold running water until it is separated and thawed.

Ingredient Substitution

We like the heartier flavor of the chicken thighs in this gumbo, but you can use the same amount of skinless, boneless chicken breast.

Finishing Touch

The red pepper sauce will lose its punch if it is added to the gumbo at the beginning of cooking. Pass the bottle of pepper sauce at the table instead, so everyone can add just the right amount to satisfy his or her taste buds.

3/4 pound skinless, boneless chicken thighs, cut into 1-inch pieces

1/4 pound fully cooked smoked sausage (two 5-inch sausages), chopped

2 medium stalks celery (with leaves), sliced (1 1/4 cups)

1 large carrot, chopped (3/4 cup)

1 medium onion, chopped (1/2 cup)

1 can (14 1/2 ounces) stewed tomatoes, undrained

5 cups water

2 tablespoons chicken bouillon granules

1 teaspoon dried thyme leaves

1 package (10 ounces) frozen cut okra, thawed and drained

3 cups hot cooked rice, for serving

Hot red pepper sauce

1. Mix all ingredients except okra, rice and pepper sauce in 3 1/2- to 6-quart slow cooker.

2. Cover and cook on low heat setting 7 to 8 hours or until chicken is no longer pink in center.

3. Stir in okra. Cover and cook on low heat setting 20 minutes.

4. Spoon rice into individual soup bowls; top with gumbo. Serve with pepper sauce.

1 Serving: Calories 270 (Calories from Fat 80); Fat 9g (Saturated 3g); Cholesterol 35mg; Sodium 1750mg; Carbohydrate 35g (Dietary Fiber 3g); Protein 15g

% Daily Value: Vitamin A 24%; Vitamin C 14%; Calcium 10%; Iron 14%

Diet Exchanges: 2 Starch, 1 Lean Meat, 1 Vegetable, 1 Fat

Fresh Vegetable-Beef Barley Soup

■ *10 servings* ■

SLOW COOKER:
3 1/2- to 6-quart

PREP TIME:
20 minutes

COOK TIME:
Low 8 to 9 hours
High 4 to 5 hours

1 1/2 pounds beef stew meat

1 small bell pepper, chopped (1/2 cup)

3/4 cup 1-inch pieces green beans

3/4 cup chopped onion

2/3 cup uncooked barley

2/3 cup fresh whole kernel corn

1 1/2 cups water

1 teaspoon salt

1 teaspoon chopped fresh or 1/2 teaspoon dried thyme leaves

1/4 teaspoon pepper

2 cans (14 1/2 ounces each) ready-to-serve beef broth

2 cans (14 1/2 ounces each) diced tomatoes with garlic, undrained

1 can (8 ounces) tomato sauce

1. Mix all ingredients in 3 1/2- to 6-quart slow cooker.

2. Cover and cook on low heat setting 8 to 9 hours (or high heat setting 4 to 5 hours) or until vegetables and barley are tender.

1 Serving: Calories 200 (Calories from Fat 65); Fat 7g (Saturated 3g); Cholesterol 35mg; Sodium 1000mg; Carbohydrate 22g (Dietary Fiber 4g); Protein 16g

% Daily Value: Vitamin A 6%; Vitamin C 16%; Calcium 4%; Iron 14%

Diet Exchanges: 1 Starch, 1 1/2 Medium-Fat Meat, 1 Vegetable

Betty's Success Tip

Select lean stew meat, or trim the extra fat before adding the beef to the soup. Trimming will take a little bit of time, but the result will be worth it since you won't have to spend time later skimming off fat.

Ingredient Substitution

If you can't find the canned diced tomatoes with garlic, use 2 cans diced tomatoes and add 1/2 teaspoon garlic powder. To save time and to make this hearty soup in the winter months, use 3/4 cup frozen cut green beans and 2/3 cup frozen whole kernel corn. Rinse the frozen vegetables under cold running water to separate and partially thaw them before adding to the soup.

Finishing Touch

Top this soup with a handful of herb-flavored croutons and a little shredded Parmesan cheese. Bursting with big, juicy chunks of meat, hearty barley and yummy vegetables, this soup is a meal in itself!

Fresh Vegetable-Beef Barley Soup ➤

Savory Cabbage and Pork Soup

■ *8 servings* ■

Slow Cooker:
3 1/2- to 6-quart

Prep Time:
20 minutes

Cook Time:
Low 8 to 9 hours
High 4 to 5 hours

Betty's Success Tip

Trimming the extra fat from the pork before cutting into pieces will give you a soup that is rich in flavor but not in fat.

Ingredient Substitution

If you like a slightly thicker soup, use two 14 1/2-ounce cans of ready-to-serve chicken broth instead of the water and bouillon cubes. If beef is your preference, use a pound of lean beef stew meat, cut into 1-inch pieces, and beef bouillon or broth instead of the pork and chicken broth.

Finishing Touch

Top each serving with a dollop of sour cream for a nice touch of creamy flavor.

1 pound boneless country-style pork ribs, cut into 1-inch pieces

4 medium carrots, cut into 1/4-inch slices (2 cups)

2 medium stalks celery, chopped (1 cup)

1 medium potato, peeled and cut into 1/2 × 1/4-inch pieces

1 medium onion, chopped (1/2 cup)

4 cups chopped cabbage (about 1 medium head)

1/4 cup packed brown sugar

4 cups water

1 teaspoon crushed red pepper

1/2 teaspoon salt

1/2 teaspoon pepper

4 chicken bouillon cubes

1 can (28 ounces) crushed tomatoes, undrained

1. Mix all ingredients in 3 1/2- to 6-quart slow cooker.

2. Cover and cook on low heat setting 8 to 9 hours (or high heat setting 4 to 5 hours) or until pork and vegetables are tender.

1 Serving: Calories 215 (Calories from Fat 65); Fat 7g (Saturated 2g); Cholesterol 35mg; Sodium 920mg; Carbohydrate 21g (Dietary Fiber 4g); Protein 14g

% Daily Value: Vitamin A 54%; Vitamin C 28%; Calcium 8%; Iron 8%

Diet Exchanges: 1 Starch, 1 High-Fat Meat, 1 Vegetable

Oriental Pork Soup

■ 6 servings ■

SLOW COOKER:
3 1/2- to 6-quart

PREP TIME:
15 minutes

COOK TIME:
Low 7 to 9 hours
High 3 to 4 hours

FINISHING COOK TIME:
Low 1 hour

1 pound chow mein meat

2 medium carrots, cut into julienne strips (1 cup)

4 medium green onions, cut into 1-inch pieces (1/4 cup)

1 clove garlic, finely chopped

1/4 cup soy sauce

1/2 teaspoon finely chopped gingerroot

1/8 teaspoon pepper

1 can (49 1/2 ounces) ready-to-serve chicken broth

1 cup sliced mushrooms

1 cup bean sprouts

1. Cook chow mein meat in 10-inch skillet over medium heat 8 to 10 minutes, stirring occasionally, until brown; drain.

2. Mix meat and remaining ingredients except mushrooms and bean sprouts in 3 1/2- to 6-quart slow cooker.

3. Cover and cook on low heat setting 7 to 9 hours (or high heat setting 3 to 4 hours).

4. Stir in mushrooms and bean sprouts.

5. Cover and cook on low heat setting about 1 hour or until mushrooms are tender.

1 Serving: Calories 220 (Calories from Fat 115); Fat 13g (Saturated 4g); Cholesterol 50mg; Sodium 1720mg; Carbohydrate 6g (Dietary Fiber 1g); Protein 21g

% Daily Value: Vitamin A 28%; Vitamin C 4%; Calcium 4%; Iron 10%

Diet Exchanges: 3 Lean Meat, 1 Vegetable, 1 Fat

Betty's Success Tip

Julienne carrots are matchlike sticks of carrots that add an interesting shape to this soup. But to save a little time, you can cut the carrots into 1/4-inch slices.

Ingredient Substitution

Coarsely ground fresh pork is sometimes labeled "chow mein meat." If it isn't available at your store, use regular ground pork, chicken or turkey. Drained canned sliced mushrooms and bean sprouts come in handy when you don't have the fresh on hand.

Finishing Touch

Spoon a mound of hot cooked rice into each bowl of soup before serving, and sprinkle with some sliced green onion tops.

Oriental Pork Soup ➤

Savory Lentil and Canadian Bacon Soup

■ 8 servings ■

SLOW COOKER:
3 1/2- to 6-quart

PREP TIME:
20 minutes

COOK TIME:
Low 8 to 9 hours
High 3 to 5 hours

Betty's Success Tip

Lentils are ideal for cooking in a slow cooker because they don't require soaking as do most dried beans and peas. The grayish green lentils are most familiar, but look for other colors such as white, yellow and red for something a little different.

Ingredient Substitution

Canadian-style bacon is a closer kin to ham than it is to regular bacon. It's taken from the lean, tender eye of the loin so it is also lower in fat, and it is fully cooked. If you have leftover ham, go ahead and use 1 1/2 cups of it for the package of Canadian-style bacon.

1 package (16 ounces) dried lentils (2 1/4 cups), sorted and rinsed

2 cans (14 1/2 ounces each) ready-to-serve vegetable broth

1 package (6 ounces) sliced Canadian-style bacon, coarsely chopped

2 medium carrots, cut into 1/2-inch pieces (1 cup)

1 medium potato, peeled and cut into 1/2-inch pieces (1 cup)

1 medium onion, chopped (1/2 cup)

1 medium stalk celery, cut into 1/2-inch pieces (1/2 cup)

4 cups water

1 teaspoon dried thyme leaves

1/2 teaspoon salt

1/4 teaspoon pepper

1. Mix all ingredients in 3 1/2- to 6-quart slow cooker.

2. Cover and cook on low heat setting 8 to 9 hours (or high heat setting 3 to 5 hours) or until lentils are tender. Stir well before serving.

1 Serving: Calories 200 (Calories from Fat 20); Fat 2g (Saturated 1g); Cholesterol 10mg; Sodium 880mg; Carbohydrate 39g (Dietary Fiber 13g); Protein 19g

% Daily Value: Vitamin A 30%; Vitamin C 6%; Calcium 4%; Iron 32%

Diet Exchanges: 1 Starch, 1 Lean Meat, 4 Vegetable

Italian Veal and Cannellini Bean Soup

■ 6 servings ■

SLOW COOKER:
3 1/2- to 6-quart

PREP TIME:
15 minutes

COOK TIME:
Low 8 to 10 hours
High 4 to 5 hours

FINISHING COOK TIME:
High 15 minutes

Betty's Success Tip

Use larger basil leaves to cut into thin strips. Stack some leaves of similar size, and roll them up starting at a long side. Cut the roll of leaves crosswise into thin strips, using a sharp knife.

Ingredient Substitution

This Italian-influenced soup can be made with pork instead of veal. Be sure to trim all the extra fat from the pork before cutting into 1-inch pieces. In a hurry? Use 1 1/2 teaspoons of lemon pepper seasoning in place of the grated lemon peel, salt and pepper.

1 1/2 pounds veal stew meat, cut into 1-inch pieces

3 medium stalks celery, cut into 1/4-inch slices (1 1/2 cups)

1 clove garlic, finely chopped

1 can (19 ounces) cannellini beans, rinsed and drained

1 can (14 1/2 ounces) ready-to-serve chicken broth

1 teaspoon grated lemon peel

1 tablespoon lemon juice

1 teaspoon salt

1/4 teaspoon pepper

1 medium red bell pepper, chopped (1 cup)

1/4 cup lightly packed fresh basil leaves, cut into thin strips

1. Mix all ingredients except bell pepper and basil in 3 1/2- to 6-quart slow cooker.

2. Cover and cook on low heat setting 8 to 10 hours (or high heat setting 4 to 5 hours) or until veal is tender.

3. Stir in bell pepper and basil.

4. Cover and cook on high heat setting about 15 minutes or until hot.

1 Serving: Calories 235 (Calories from Fat 45); Fat 5g (Saturated 2g); Cholesterol 70mg; Sodium 790mg; Carbohydrate 25g (Dietary Fiber 6g); Protein 28g

% Daily Value: Vitamin A 2%; Vitamin C 16%; Calcium 12%; Iron 24%

Diet Exchanges: 1 Starch, 3 Very Lean Meat, 2 Vegetable

Multi-Bean Soup

■ 12 servings ■

SLOW COOKER:
5 to 6-quart

PREP TIME:
10 minutes

COOK TIME:
High 8 to 10 hours

FINISHING COOK TIME:
High 15 minutes

Betty's Success Tip

The shredded carrots are added at the end so they don't overcook and disappear into the soup. Also, the tomatoes are added after the beans are tender because the acid in the tomatoes can prevent the beans from becoming tender during the long, slow cooking.

Ingredient Substitution

Have small amounts of various leftover dried beans in your cupboard? Mix them together to make 2 1/4 cups of beans, and use them instead of purchasing a package of bean soup mix. Or use a 16-ounce package of dried beans for the bean soup mix, but use only 8 cups of water and 3/4 teaspoon salt.

Finishing Touch

Add a secret ingredient to this soup for additional flavor and color—stir in 1 cup canned pumpkin when you add the carrots and tomatoes.

1 package (20 ounces) 15- or 16-dried bean soup mix, sorted and rinsed

1/2 pound smoked beef sausage ring, cut into 1/4-inch slices

1 large onion, chopped (1 cup)

10 cups water

1 1/2 teaspoons dried thyme leaves

1 teaspoon salt

1/2 teaspoon pepper

2 medium carrots, shredded (1 1/3 cups)

1 can (14 1/2 ounces) diced tomatoes, undrained

1. Mix all ingredients except carrots and tomatoes in 5- to 6-quart slow cooker.

2. Cover and cook on high heat setting 8 to 10 hours or until beans are tender.

3. Stir in carrots and tomatoes.

4. Cover and cook on high heat setting about 15 minutes or until hot.

1 Serving: Calories 210 (Calories from Fat 55); Fat 6g (Saturated 3g); Cholesterol 10mg; Sodium 660mg; Carbohydrate 35g (Dietary Fiber 6g); Protein 10g

% Daily Value: Vitamin A 22%; Vitamin C 10%; Calcium 4%; Iron 14%

Diet Exchanges: 2 Starch, 1/2 Lean Meat, 1 Vegetable

Easy Beans and Frank Soup

■ 6 servings ■

SLOW COOKER:
3 1/2- to 6-quart

PREP TIME:
10 minutes

COOK TIME:
Low 6 to 8 hours
High 3 to 4 hours

Ingredient Substitution

The eight-vegetable juice adds a nice spicy flavor to this easy-to-make soup. For an all-family-appeal soup, however, you may want to use tomato juice instead of the eight-vegetable juice.

Serving Suggestion

For a super-easy and nutritious meal, serve this protein-packed soup with crisp carrot and celery sticks, and pass a bowl of bright red apples for dessert.

Finishing Touch

Add a little fun by sprinkling shredded mozzarella cheese on top of each bowl of hot soup. The kids will love the way it "strings" when they spoon into it. Or top with a slice of process American cheese or some shredded Cheddar cheese—it won't string, but it will add flavor.

1 can (28 ounces) baked beans with bacon and brown sugar sauce, undrained

1 can (11 1/2 ounces) eight-vegetable juice

6 franks or hot dogs, cut into 1-inch slices

3 medium carrots, chopped (1 1/2 cups)

1 large onion, chopped (1 cup)

1 clove garlic, finely chopped

1 teaspoon Worcestershire sauce

1. Mix all ingredients in 3 1/2- to 6-quart slow cooker.

2. Cover and cook on low heat setting 6 to 8 hours (or high heat setting 3 to 4 hours) or until carrots are tender.

1 Serving: Calories 295 (Calories from Fat 135); Fat 14g (Saturated 5g); Cholesterol 25mg; Sodium 1370mg; Carbohydrate 34g (Dietary Fiber 8g); Protein 14g

% Daily Value: Vitamin A 54%; Vitamin C 18%; Calcium 8%; Iron 16%

Diet Exchanges: 2 Starch, 1 High-Fat Meat, 1 Vegetable

Lima Bean and Kielbasa Soup

■ *12 servings* ■

Crowd
S I Z E

SLOW COOKER:
5 to 6-quart

PREP TIME:
15 minutes

COOK TIME:
High 10 to 12 hours

FINISHING COOK TIME:
15 minutes

Betty's Success Tip

Kielbasa is a smoked sausage that is usually made of pork but sometimes has beef added. "Kielbasa," "kielbasy" or "Polish sausage" are all names for this flavorful sausage. Use turkey kielbasa for a lower-fat soup.

Ingredient Substitution

You can used other dried beans for the limas, such as great Northern, navy, kidney or cannellini beans, and the cooking time will not change. Or use 2 cups of mixed dried beans by mixing different beans together to add a variety of shapes and color to the soup.

Serving Suggestion

This recipe makes a big batch. Enjoy a meal now and freeze the remaining soup for later. If you freeze it in an airtight container, it will keep up to a month. When your mouth is watering for kielbasa and bean soup, just thaw it in the refrigerator and heat it.

1 package (16 ounces) dried lima beans, sorted and rinsed

1 pound kielbasa sausage, cut into 1/4-inch slices

2 medium carrots, cut into 1/4-inch slices (1 cup)

2 medium stalks celery, cut into 1/4-inch slices (1 cup)

1 large onion, chopped (1 cup)

2 cloves garlic, finely chopped

6 cups water

1 teaspoon salt

1/2 teaspoon pepper

1 can (14 1/2 ounces) diced tomatoes, undrained

1. Mix all ingredients except tomatoes in 5- to 6-quart slow cooker.

2. Cover and cook on high heat setting 10 to 12 hours or until beans are tender.

3. Stir in tomatoes.

4. Cover and cook on high heat setting about 15 minutes or until hot.

1 Serving: Calories 215 (Calories from Fat 100); Fat 11g (Saturated 4g); Cholesterol 20mg; Sodium 650mg; Carbohydrate 24g (Dietary Fiber 7g); Protein 12g

% Daily Value: Vitamin A 18%; Vitamin C 6%; Calcium 4%; Iron 16%

Diet Exchanges: 1 Starch, 1 High-Fat Meat, 2 Vegetable

Squash and Apple Bisque

8 servings

SLOW COOKER:
3 1/2- to 6-quart

PREP TIME:
15 minutes

COOK TIME:
Low 8 to 10 hours
High 3 to 5 hours

FINISHING COOK TIME:
Low 15 minutes

1 butternut squash (2 pounds), peeled and cubed

1 medium onion, chopped (1/2 cup)

1 can (14 1/2 ounces) ready-to-serve chicken broth

2 cups applesauce

1/2 teaspoon ground ginger

1/4 teaspoon salt

1 cup sour cream

1. Mix all ingredients except sour cream in 3 1/2- to 6-quart slow cooker.

2. Cover and cook on low heat setting 8 to 10 hours (or high heat setting 3 to 5 hours) or until squash is tender.

3. Place one-third to one-half of the mixture at a time in blender or food processor. Cover and blend on high speed until smooth. Return mixture to cooker.

4. Stir in sour cream. Cover and cook on low heat setting 15 minutes or just until soup is hot; stir.

5. Garnish each serving with a dollop of sour cream.

Betty's Success Tip

Sour cream will break down and curdle if it is heated too long or becomes too hot. After adding the cold sour cream, cook the bisque just long enough for it to reheat. If you use reduced-fat sour cream, add it the same way.

Serving Suggestion

For a delightful taste treat, serve this bisque thoroughly chilled. Garnish with thin slices of Granny Smith apples and a sprinkling of finely chopped crystallized ginger.

Finishing Touch

Spoon a dollop of sour cream on top of each serving, then swirl slightly into the soup with the tip of a knife. For a touch of crunch and color, sprinkle with poppy seed or chopped pecans.

1 Serving: Calories 140 (Calories from Fat 55); Fat 6g (Saturated 4g); Cholesterol 20mg; Sodium 330mg; Carbohydrate 19g (Dietary Fiber 2g); Protein 3g

% Daily Value: Vitamin A 70%; Vitamin C 12%; Calcium 6%; Iron 4%

Diet Exchanges: 1 Starch, 1 Vegetable, 1 Fat

Potato and Double Corn Chowder

■ 6 servings ■

SLOW COOKER:
3 1/2- to 6-quart

PREP TIME:
15 minutes

COOK TIME:
Low 6 to 8 hours
High 3 to 4 hours

1 bag (16 ounces) frozen hash brown potatoes, thawed (4 cups)

1 can (15 1/4 ounces) whole kernel corn, undrained

1 can (14 3/4 ounces) cream-style corn

1 can (12 ounces) evaporated milk

1 medium onion, chopped (1/2 cup)

8 slices bacon, cooked and crumbled

1/2 teaspoon salt

1/2 teaspoon Worcestershire sauce

1/4 teaspoon pepper

Ingredient Substitution

A great way to use leftover cut-up cooked turkey or chicken is to add it to this chowder for a hearty one-dish meal. Or use cut-up fully cooked ham instead of cooking and crumbling bacon.

Finishing Touch

The bacon adds that good smoky flavor, but it does lose its crispness when added at the beginning. If you like the crisp texture of bacon, stir the bacon in at the end of the cooking instead. Also, sprinkle the chowder with some chopped fresh parsley for added color.

1. Mix all ingredients in 3 1/2- to 6-quart slow cooker.

2. Cover and cook on low heat setting 6 to 8 hours (or high heat setting 3 to 4 hours) to develop flavors.

1 Serving: Calories 305 (Calories from Fat 65); Fat 7g (Saturated 2g); Cholesterol 12mg; Sodium 1040mg; Carbohydrate 55g (Dietary Fiber 5g); Protein 11g

% Daily Value: Vitamin A 12%; Vitamin C 18%; Calcium 10%; Iron 10%

Diet Exchanges: 3 Starch, 2 Vegetable, 1 Fat

Peppery Fish Chowder with Rice

■ 10 servings ■

SLOW COOKER:
3 1/2- to 6-quart

PREP TIME:
15 minutes

COOK TIME:
Low 7 to 9 hours
High 3 to 4 hours

FINISHING COOK TIME:
High 30 to 45 minutes

Betty's Success Tip

Cutting the fish into 1-inch pieces will be a snap if you use fish steaks that are 1 inch thick or use thicker cuts of fish fillets. Any firm-fleshed fish, such as halibut, haddock, swordfish, pollack, tuna or red snapper, works well in this soup. If fish is frozen, thaw it in the refrigerator or under cold running water before cutting it into pieces and adding it to the soup.

Ingredient Substitution

The red cayenne pepper in this chowder packs a little punch, but if you prefer a chowder that's a little more tame, use black pepper instead. If you like really fiery chowder, pass a bottle of red pepper sauce at the table!

2 medium stalks celery, chopped (1 cup)

1 medium bell pepper, chopped (1 cup)

1 medium onion, chopped (1/2 cup)

2 cloves garlic, finely chopped

2 cans (14 1/2 ounces each) diced tomatoes, undrained

1/2 cup uncooked instant rice

2 cups eight-vegetable juice

1 cup dry white wine or vegetable broth

1 tablespoon Worcestershire sauce

1 teaspoon salt

1/4 teaspoon ground red pepper (cayenne)

1 pound firm-fleshed fish steak, cut into 1-inch pieces

3 tablespoons chopped fresh parsley

1. Mix all ingredients except fish and parsley in 3 1/2- to 6-quart slow cooker.

2. Cover and cook on low heat setting 7 to 9 hours (or high heat setting 3 to 4 hours) or until rice is tender.

3. Stir in fish and parsley.

4. Cover and cook on high heat setting 30 to 45 minutes or until fish flakes easily with fork.

1 Serving: Calories 90 (Calories from Fat 10); Fat 1g (Saturated 0g); Cholesterol 20mg; Sodium 540mg; Carbohydrate 13g (Dietary Fiber 2g); Protein 9g

% Daily Value: Vitamin A 12%; Vitamin C 32%; Calcium 4%; Iron 6%

Diet Exchanges: 1 Starch, 1 Very Lean Meat

Chicken Stew with Pepper and Pineapple

■ *4 servings* ■

SLOW COOKER:
3 1/2- to 6-quart

PREP TIME:
20 minutes

COOK TIME:
Low 7 to 8 hours
High 3 to 4 hours

FINISHING COOK TIME:
High 15 minutes

Ingredient Substitution

If you don't have fresh gingerroot, no problem! Just use 1 teaspoon ground ginger in place of it.

Finishing Touch

To be sure you get every last drop of the yummy gingery-flavored sauce, spoon the stew over hot cooked rice. To turn a great stew into an extra-special stew, just sprinkle with sliced green onions and toasted coconut or chopped peanuts or cashews.

1 pound skinless, boneless chicken breasts, cut into 1 1/2-inch pieces

4 medium carrots, cut into 1-inch pieces

1/2 cup chicken broth

2 tablespoons finely chopped gingerroot

1 tablespoon packed brown sugar

2 tablespoons soy sauce

1/2 teaspoon ground allspice

1/2 teaspoon red pepper sauce

1 can (8 ounces) pineapple chunks in juice, drained and juice reserved

1 tablespoon cornstarch

1 medium bell pepper, cut into 1-inch pieces

1. Mix all ingredients except pineapple, cornstarch and bell pepper in 3 1/2- to 6-quart slow cooker.

2. Cover and cook on low heat setting 7 to 8 hours (or high heat setting 3 to 4 hours) or until vegetables are tender and chicken is no longer pink in center.

3. Mix reserved pineapple juice and cornstarch until smooth; gradually stir into chicken mixture. Stir in pineapple and bell pepper.

4. Cover and cook on high heat setting about 15 minutes or until slightly thickened.

1 Serving: Calories 225 (Calories from Fat 30); Fat 4g (Saturated 1g); Cholesterol 70mg; Sodium 690mg; Carbohydrate 24g (Dietary Fiber 3g); Protein 27g

% Daily Value: Vitamin A 96%; Vitamin C 32%; Calcium 4%; Iron 10%

Diet Exchanges: 3 1/2 Very Lean Meat, 2 Vegetable, 1 Fruit

Chicken Stew with Pepper and Pineapple ➤

Brunswick Stew

■ 10 servings ■

Crowd
SIZE

SLOW COOKER:
3 1/2- to 6-quart

PREP TIME:
20 minutes

COOK TIME:
Low 8 to 10 hours
High 3 to 4 hours

Betty's Success Tip

Traditionally, Brunswick Stew is made with whole kernel corn, but we like the creaminess that the cream-style corn gives this southern favorite. Be sure to cut the potatoes into 1/2-inch pieces, so they will be tender when the stew is done cooking.

Ingredient Substitution

Lima is the popular bean for this stew, but a drained 16-ounce can of butter beans gives the same great results.

Serving Suggestion

Brunswick Stew is a popular classic from Virginia's Brunswick County, hence its name. This hearty stew originally was made of squirrel and onion, but today chicken is the more popular meat of choice. Warm baking powder biscuits slathered with butter, another southern favorite, will be all you need for a satisfying meal.

1 1/2 pounds skinless, boneless chicken breasts, cut into 1-inch pieces

3 medium potatoes, cut into 1/2-inch pieces

1 medium onion, chopped (1/2 cup)

1 can (28 ounces) crushed tomatoes, undrained

1 can (15 to 16 ounces) lima beans, rinsed and drained

1 can (14 3/4 ounces) cream-style corn

1 tablespoon Worcestershire sauce

3/4 teaspoon salt

1/2 teaspoon dried marjoram leaves

8 slices bacon, cooked and crumbled

1/4 teaspoon red pepper sauce

1. Mix all ingredients except bacon and pepper sauce in 3 1/2- to 6-quart slow cooker.

2. Cover and cook on low heat setting 8 to 10 hours (or high heat setting 3 to 4 hours) or until potatoes are tender.

3. Stir in bacon and pepper sauce.

1 Serving: Calories 250 (Calories from Fat 55); Fat 6g (Saturated 2g); Cholesterol 50mg; Sodium 630mg; Carbohydrate 31g (Dietary Fiber 6g); Protein 24g

% Daily Value: Vitamin A 6%; Vitamin C 16%; Calcium 4%; Iron 16%

Diet Exchanges: 1 Starch, 2 Lean Meat, 3 Vegetable

Sausage Gumbo

■ *8 servings* ■

Slow Cooker:
3 1/2- to 6-quart

Prep Time:
15 minutes

Cook Time:
Low 7 to 9 hours
High 3 to 4 hours

Finishing Cook Time:
High 30 minutes

Betty's Success Tip

Okra not only adds flavor, but as it cooks it helps to thicken the gumbo sauce. It's a popular vegetable throughout the South and is a signature ingredient for gumbos. In fact, the name gumbo is a derivation of the African word for "okra." This vegetable was brought to the South from Africa.

Ingredient Substitution

Some gumbos are made with a variety of meats instead of just sausage. Cut 1/2 pound of skinless, boneless chicken breasts or thighs, beef round steak or ham into 1/2-inch pieces, and add with 1/2 pound of sliced sausage. Or use a little of each to equal a pound of meat.

Finishing Touch

Adding greens to your gumbo is a symbol for good luck. Place about 4 cups of fresh spinach on top of the cooked gumbo. Cover the cooker and let it stand about 10 minutes or until the spinach is wilted. Stir the spinach into the gumbo before serving.

1 pound fully cooked smoked sausage, cut into 1/2-inch slices

1 medium green bell pepper, chopped (1 cup)

1 medium onion, chopped (1/2 cup)

2 cloves garlic, finely chopped

1 can (28 ounces) crushed tomatoes, undrained

1 tablespoon Worcestershire sauce

1/4 teaspoon salt

1/4 teaspoon pepper

1 package (10 ounces) frozen sliced okra, thawed and drained

1 tablespoon white vinegar

1/4 to 1/2 teaspoon red pepper sauce

4 cups hot cooked rice, for serving

1. Mix sausage, bell pepper, onion, garlic, tomatoes, Worcestershire sauce, salt and pepper in 3 1/2- to 6-quart slow cooker.

2. Cover and cook on low heat setting 7 to 9 hours (or high heat setting 3 to 4 hours) or until vegetables are tender.

3. Stir in okra, vinegar and pepper sauce.

4. Cover and cook on high heat setting about 30 minutes or until slightly thickened.

5. Serve gumbo over rice.

1 Serving: Calories 305 (Calories from Fat 145); Fat 16g (Saturated 6g); Cholesterol 30mg; Sodium 820mg; Carbohydrate 32g (Dietary Fiber 3g); Protein 11g

% Daily Value: Vitamin A 8%; Vitamin C 26%; Calcium 8%; Iron 14%

Diet Exchanges: 2 Starch, 1 High-Fat Meat, 1 Fat

Jambalaya

■ 8 servings ■

SLOW COOKER:
3 1/2- to 6-quart

PREP TIME:
20 minutes

COOK TIME:
Low 7 to 8 hours
High 3 to 4 hours

FINISHING COOK TIME:
Low 1 hour

Ingredient Substitution

Andouille sausage, which is a spicy, heavily smoked sausage, is the traditional sausage for jambalaya. Any sausage will taste good, however, and a smoked turkey sausage will add flavor but not as much fat as regular sausage. Have leftover ham in the refrigerator? Use the same amount of ham for the sausage.

Serving Suggestion

Here's a fun way of serving rice. Spray the inside of a 1/2-cup measuring cup with cooking spray. For each serving, press the hot rice into the cup. Place the cup upside down in the bottom of a bowl and unmold the rice. Spoon the jambalaya around the mound of rice. Serve with warm crusty bread.

Finishing Touch

If you prefer more "heat," sprinkle additional red pepper sauce on this Cajun favorite just before serving. If you want to use fresh parsley and thyme, add them with the shrimp so the flavor isn't lost during the long cooking.

1 large onion, chopped (1 cup)

1 medium green bell pepper, chopped (1 cup)

2 medium stalks celery, chopped (1 cup)

3 cloves garlic, finely chopped

1 can (28 ounces) diced tomatoes, undrained

2 cups chopped fully cooked smoked sausage

1 tablespoon parsley flakes

1/2 teaspoon dried thyme leaves

1/2 teaspoon salt

1/4 teaspoon pepper

1/4 teaspoon red pepper sauce

3/4 pound uncooked peeled deveined medium shrimp, thawed if frozen

4 cups hot cooked rice, for serving

1. Mix all ingredients except shrimp and rice in 3 1/2- to 6-quart slow cooker.

2. Cover and cook on low heat setting 7 to 8 hours (or high heat setting 3 to 4 hours) or until vegetables are tender.

3. Stir in shrimp. Cover and cook on low heat setting about 1 hour or until shrimp are pink and firm.

4. Serve jambalaya with rice.

1 Serving: Calories 255 (Calories from Fat 90); Fat 10g (Saturated 4g); Cholesterol 60mg; Sodium 710mg; Carbohydrate 31g (Dietary Fiber 2g); Protein 12g

% Daily Value: Vitamin A 8%; Vitamin C 28%; Calcium 6%; Iron 16%

Diet Exchanges: 2 Starch, 1 High-Fat Meat

Jambalaya ➤

Beef Stew with Sun-Dried Tomatoes

■ 6 servings ■

Slow Cooker:
3 1/2- to 6-quart

Prep Time:
20 minutes

Cook Time:
Low 8 to 9 hours
High 3 to 5 hours

Finishing Cook Time:
High 10 to 15 minutes

Betty's Success Tip

Purchased stew meat does save time, but other cuts of beef also work well for this stew. Try chuck, tip or top or bottom round steak. Get a 1-inch-thick piece of boneless steak, trim the extra fat and cut the steak into 1-inch pieces.

Ingredient Substitution

Sun-dried tomatoes, or dried tomatoes, add a nice concentrated tomato flavor to the stew. When fresh tomatoes are plentiful, you can add 2 cups chopped fresh tomatoes with the flour mixture instead of using the dried tomatoes.

Finishing Touch

Serve stew in bowls, and sprinkle each serving with crumbled crisply cooked bacon and chopped fresh parsley.

1 cup sun-dried tomatoes (not oil-packed)

1 1/2 pounds beef stew meat

12 medium new potatoes (1 1/2 pounds), cut in half

1 medium onion, cut into 8 wedges

1 bag (8 ounces) baby-cut carrots (about 30)

2 cups water

1 1/2 teaspoons seasoned salt

1 bay leaf

1/4 cup cold water

2 tablespoons all-purpose flour

1. Soak tomatoes in water as directed on package; drain and coarsely chop.

2. Mix tomatoes and remaining ingredients except 1/4 cup water and the flour in 3 1/2- to 6-quart slow cooker.

3. Cover and cook on low heat setting 8 to 9 hours (or high heat setting 3 to 5 hours) or until beef and vegetables are tender.

4. Mix 1/4 cup water and the flour; gradually stir into beef mixture.

5. Cover and cook on high heat setting 10 to 15 minutes or until slightly thickened. Remove bay leaf.

1 Serving: Calories 310 (Calories from Fat 100); Fat 11g (Saturated 4g); Cholesterol 60mg; Sodium 600mg; Carbohydrate 34g (Dietary Fiber 5g); Protein 24g

% Daily Value: Vitamin A 78%; Vitamin C 16%; Calcium 4%; Iron 24%

Diet Exchanges: 2 Starch, 2 Lean Meat, 1 Vegetable, 1/2 Fat

Beef Stew with Sun-Dried Tomatoes ➤

Burgundy Stew with Herb Dumplings

■ *8 servings* ■

SLOW COOKER:
3 1/2- to 6-quart

PREP TIME:
25 minutes

COOK TIME:
Low 8 to 10 hours
High 4 to 5 hours

FINISHING COOK TIME:
High 25 to 35 minutes

Betty's Success Tip

To make fluffy dumplings, drop the dumpling dough on the stew pieces rather than directly into the liquid. The dumplings will steam rather than settle into the liquid and become soggy. Also, be sure the stew is piping hot, so the dumplings will start to cook from the steam right away and become fluffy.

Ingredient Substitution

Save time cleaning and slicing carrots, and use 2 cups of baby-cut carrots instead. Keeping a bag of ready-to-eat baby-cut carrots in the refrigerator is handy for nibbling on or to have ready to put into soups or stews.

Serving Suggestion

Want to save some time by not making the dumplings? Instead, just serve the stew in bowls with big chunks of crusty Italian bread for dipping into the stew and soaking up all the delicious wine-flavored broth.

2 pounds beef boneless bottom or top round, cut into 1-inch pieces

4 medium carrots, cut into 1/4-inch slices (2 cups)

2 medium stalks celery, sliced (1 cup)

2 medium onions, sliced

1 can (14 1/2 ounces) diced tomatoes, undrained

1 can (8 ounces) sliced mushrooms, drained

3/4 cup dry red wine or beef broth

1 1/2 teaspoons salt

1 teaspoon dried thyme leaves

1 teaspoon ground mustard (dry)

1/4 teaspoon pepper

1/4 cup water

3 tablespoons all-purpose flour

Herb Dumplings (below)

1. Mix all ingredients except water, flour and Herb Dumplings in 3 1/2- to 6-quart slow cooker.

2. Cover and cook on low heat setting 8 to 10 hours (or high heat setting 4 to 5 hours) or until vegetables and beef are tender. Mix water and flour; gradually stir into beef mixture.

3. Prepare Herb Dumplings. Drop dough by spoonfuls onto hot beef mixture. Cover and cook on high heat setting 25 to 35 minutes or until toothpick inserted in center of dumplings comes out clean.

Herb Dumplings

Mix 1 1/2 cups Bisquick® Original baking mix, 1/2 teaspoon dried thyme leaves, and 1/4 teaspoon dried sage leaves, crumbled. Stir in 1/2 cup milk just until baking mix is moistened.

1 Serving: Calories 255 (Calories from Fat 65); Fat 7g (Saturated 2g); Cholesterol 55mg; Sodium 1030mg; Carbohydrate26g (Dietary Fiber 3g); Protein 25g

% Daily Value: Vitamin A 50%; Vitamin C 10%; Calcium 10%; Iron 20%

Diet Exchanges: 1 Starch, 2 Lean Meat, 2 Vegetable

Irish Stew

■ 8 servings ■

SLOW COOKER:
3 1/2- to 6-quart

PREP TIME:
15 minutes

COOK TIME:
Low 8 to 10 hours
High 3 to 5 hours

Ingredient Substitution

This stew also can be made with 2 pounds of lean beef stew meat instead of the lamb. It is so easy, you will want to make it an everyday favorite.

Serving Suggestion

Plan to serve this stew on a Saturday or Sunday evening. Take the time to bake a loaf of Irish soda bread, using your favorite recipe. Complete the meal with tall glasses of full-bodied stout beer. This meal is so good, it will put you in the mood to dance a jig!

Finishing Touch

Like green peas in your Irish stew? Thaw a cup of frozen green peas, or rinse them under cold running water until separated and thawed. Stir them into the stew after you have skimmed off the fat, and let the heat of the stew warm the peas.

2 pounds lean lamb stew meat

6 medium potatoes (2 pounds), cut into 1/2-inch slices

3 medium onions, sliced

1 teaspoon salt

1/4 teaspoon pepper

1 teaspoon dried thyme leaves

1 can (14 1/2 ounces) ready-to-serve beef broth

Chopped fresh parsley, if desired

1. Layer half each of the lamb, potatoes and onions in 3 1/2- to 6-quart slow cooker. Sprinkle with half each of the salt, pepper and thyme. Repeat layers and sprinkle with remaining seasonings. Pour broth over top.

2. Cover and cook on low heat setting 8 to 10 hours (or high heat setting 3 to 5 hours) or until lamb and vegetables are tender.

3. Skim fat from stew. Sprinkle parsley over stew.

1 Serving: Calories 250 (Calories from Fat 65); Fat 7g (Saturated 2g); Cholesterol 60mg; Sodium 590mg; Carbohydrate 27g (Dietary Fiber 3g); Protein 23g

% Daily Value: Vitamin A 0%; Vitamin C 12%; Calcium 2%; Iron 16%

Diet Exchanges: 1 Starch, 2 Lean Meat, 2 Vegetable

Hearty Pork Stew

■ 6 servings ■

SLOW COOKER:
3 1/2- to 6-quart

PREP TIME:
25 minutes

COOK TIME:
Low 6 to 7 hours
High 3 to 4 hours

FINISHING COOK TIME:
High 30 to 45 minutes

Betty's Success Tip

Chicken broth is available in an aseptic box that is handy to use. It has an easy-to-open pour spout, and any leftover broth can be stored in the box in the refrigerator. Four cups of chicken broth or broth made from bouillon cubes or granules can be used in place of the box of broth.

Ingredient Substitution

Parsnips, that root vegetable that looks like a creamy white carrot, have a slightly sweet flavor that goes nicely with pork. However, instead of the parsnips, two more sliced carrots can be used and the stew will be just as colorful and tasty.

1 1/2 pounds pork boneless loin, cut into 1-inch cubes

3 medium carrots, cut into 1/4-inch slices (1 1/2 cups)

1 medium onion, chopped (1/2 cup)

1 box (32 ounces) ready-to-serve chicken broth

2 cups 1/2-inch diced peeled parsnips

1 1/2 cups 1-inch cubes peeled butternut squash

1/2 teaspoon salt

1/2 teaspoon pepper

3 tablespoons all-purpose flour

3 tablespoons margarine or butter, softened

1. Mix all ingredients except flour and margarine in 3 1/2- to 6-quart slow cooker.

2. Cover and cook on low heat setting 6 to 7 hours (or high heat setting 3 to 4 hours) or until pork is no longer pink and vegetables are tender.

3. Mix flour and margarine. Gently stir flour mixture, 1 spoonful at a time, into pork mixture until blended.

4. Cover and cook on high heat setting 30 to 45 minutes, stirring occasionally, until thickened.

1 Serving: Calories 275 (Calories from Fat 115); Fat 13g (Saturated 4g); Cholesterol 50mg; Sodium 1010mg; Carbohydrate 21g (Dietary Fiber 4g); Protein 23g

% Daily Value: Vitamin A 80%; Vitamin C 12%; Calcium 6%; Iron 10%

Diet Exchanges: 1 Starch, 2 1/2 Medium-Fat Meat, 1 Vegetable

Hearty Pork Stew ➤

Venison Stew

■ 8 servings ■

SLOW COOKER:
3 1/2- to 6-quart

PREP TIME:
20 minutes

COOK TIME:
Low 8 to 10 hours

FINISHING COOK TIME:
High 30 minutes

Ingredient Substitution

If you aren't "game" for venison, you still can enjoy this savory, sweet-sour-flavored stew by using the same amount of lean beef stew meat. If the chunks of beef are large, cut them into 1-inch pieces.

Serving Suggestion

Be sure to serve plenty of hearty whole-grain bread with this stew so everyone can sop up every last drop of the wonderful gravy in the bottom of the bowl!

2 pounds venison, cut into 1-inch pieces

2 medium onions, cut into 1/2-inch slices

1 pound small red potatoes, cut into 1/4-inch slices

2 medium apples, cut into 1/2-inch slices

1 bay leaf

1 can (10 1/2 ounces) condensed beef broth

1 cup red Burgundy wine or beef broth

1/2 cup Worcestershire sauce

1/2 cup packed brown sugar

1/8 teaspoon pepper

2 cloves garlic, finely chopped

1/4 cup all-purpose flour

1/4 cup water

1. Layer venison, onions, potatoes, apples and bay leaf in 31/2- to 6-quart slow cooker. Mix wine or broth, Worcestershire sauce, brown sugar, pepper and garlic; pour into cooker.

2. Cover and cook on low heat setting 8 to 10 hours or until venison is tender.

3. Mix flour and water; stir into venison mixture. Cover and cook on high heat setting about 30 minutes or until slightly thickened. Remove bay leaf.

1 Serving: Calories 285 (Calories from Fat 25); Fat 3g (Saturated 1g); Cholesterol 95mg; Sodium 310mg; Carbohydrate 39g (Dietary Fiber 3g); Protein 28g

% Daily Value: Vitamin A 0%; Vitamin C 10%; Calcium 4%; Iron 32%

Diet Exchanges: 1 Starch, 3 Very Lean Meat, 2 Vegetable, 1 Fruit

Turkey and Brown Rice Chili

6 servings

SLOW COOKER:
3 1/2- to 6-quart

PREP TIME:
15 minutes

COOK TIME:
Low 8 to 10 hours
High 4 to 5 hours

FINISHING COOK TIME:
High 15 minutes

Betty's Success Tip

This is a lower-fat chili because it is made with ground turkey breast. Make sure that you are buying ground turkey breast and not regular ground turkey, which includes both light and dark meat and will be higher in fat.

Ingredient Substitution

Have ground beef in the freezer? Use it instead of the turkey, and you won't need the oil to cook it in. Stir in either brown or white rice to finish the chili.

Finishing Touch

Enjoy this chili topped with your favorite salsa and corn chips. Like cilantro? Stir a couple of tablespoons of chopped fresh cilantro into the chili before serving.

1 tablespoon vegetable oil

3/4 pound ground turkey breast

1 large onion, chopped (1 cup)

2 cans (14 1/2 ounces each) diced tomatoes, undrained

1 can (15 or 16 ounces) chili beans in sauce, undrained

1 can (4 ounces) chopped green chilies, drained

1/2 cup water

1 tablespoon sugar

2 teaspoons chili powder

1 teaspoon ground cumin

1/2 teaspoon salt

2 cups cooked brown rice

1. Heat oil in 12-inch skillet over medium heat. Cook turkey and onion in oil, stirring frequently, until turkey is no longer pink; drain.

2. Mix turkey mixture and remaining ingredients except rice in 3 1/2- to 6-quart slow cooker.

3. Cover and cook on low heat setting 8 to 10 hours (or high heat setting 4 to 5 hours).

4. Stir in rice.

5. Cover and cook on high heat setting about 15 minutes or until rice is hot.

1 Serving: Calories 235 (Calories from Fat 30); Fat 4g (Saturated 1g); Cholesterol 40mg; Sodium 980mg; Carbohydrate 37g (Dietary Fiber 6g); Protein 20g

% Daily Value: Vitamin A 14%; Vitamin C 34%; Calcium 8%; Iron 20%

Diet Exchanges: 2 Starch, 2 Very Lean Meat, 1 Vegetable

Vegetarian Chili with Baked Tortilla Strips

◼ *6 servings* ◼

SLOW COOKER:
3 1/2- to 6-quart

PREP TIME:
15 minutes

COOK TIME:
Low 5 to 6 hours

Ingredient Substitution

Use any canned beans that you have on hand for the pinto or kidney beans. For variety, try great northern, black, garbanzo or lima beans, as well as black-eyed peas.

Serving Suggestion

This bean-packed chili is great served over hot cooked brown or white rice to make a heartier meatless meal. You decide if you want the tortilla strips on top.

Finishing Touch

For a cool zing, mix a tablespoon or two of fresh lime juice into 1 cup of sour cream to spoon on top of the chili. Sprinkle with chopped fresh cilantro or sliced green onions.

Baked Tortilla Strips (below)

1 can (15 or 16 ounces) spicy chili beans in sauce, undrained

1 can (15 to 16 ounces) pinto beans, undrained

1 can (15 to 16 ounces) dark red kidney beans, drained

1 can (14 1/2 ounces) chili-style chunky tomatoes, undrained

1 large onion, chopped (1 cup)

2 to 3 teaspoons chili powder

1/8 teaspoon ground red pepper (cayenne)

1. Prepare Baked Tortilla Strips.

2. Mix remaining ingredients in 3 1/2- to 6-quart slow cooker.

3. Cover and cook on low heat setting 5 to 6 hours or until flavors have blended.

4. Stir well before serving. Spoon chili over tortilla strips, or sprinkle tortilla strips on top.

Baked Tortilla Strips

Heat oven to 400°. Cut 2 flour tortillas (8 inches in diameter) in half; cut each half crosswise into 1/2-inch strips. Place in single layer on ungreased cookie sheet. Bake 10 to 12 minutes or until strips are crisp and edges are light brown.

1 Serving: Calories 220 (Calories from Fat 20); Fat 2g (Saturated 0g); Cholesterol 0mg; Sodium 880mg; Carbohydrate 48g (Dietary Fiber 12g); Protein 14g

% Daily Value: Vitamin A 10%; Vitamin C 16%; Calcium 10%; Iron 28%

Diet Exchanges: 2 Starch, 3 Vegetable

Vegetarian Chili with Baked Tortilla Strips ➤

Family Favorite Chili

■ 8 servings ■

Slow Cooker:
3 1/2- to 6-quart

Prep Time:
20 minutes

Cook Time:
Low 6 to 8 hours
High 3 to 4 hours

Finishing Cook Time:
High 15 to 20 minutes

Betty's Success Tip

Starting with hot cooked ground beef is safer because getting cold, uncooked ground beef to a safe temperature in a slow cooker takes too long. Also, using cooked and drained ground beef helps eliminate that extra fat and liquid that would accumulate during cooking.

Ingredient Substitution

Like a hot and spicy chili? Use a pound of ground beef and a pound of hot and spicy pork or Italian bulk sausage instead of all beef. Cook and drain the two together before adding to the cooker.

Serving Suggestion

Chili is great by itself in a bowl, and it also makes a great topper. For a Cincinnati-style treat, serve chili over hot cooked spaghetti and sprinkle with shredded Cheddar cheese and chopped onion. Kids love chili spooned on corn chips because it reminds them of a taco.

2 pounds ground beef

1 large onion, chopped (1 cup)

2 cloves garlic, finely chopped

1 can (28 ounces) diced tomatoes, undrained

1 can (15 ounces) tomato sauce

2 tablespoons chili powder

1 1/2 teaspoons ground cumin

1/2 teaspoon salt

1/2 teaspoon pepper

1 can (15 or 16 ounces) kidney or pinto beans, rinsed and drained

1. Cook beef in 12-inch skillet over medium heat, stirring occasionally, until brown; drain.

2. Mix beef and remaining ingredients except beans in 3 1/2- to 6-quart slow cooker.

3. Cover and cook on low heat setting 6 to 8 hours (or high heat setting 3 to 4 hours) or until onion is tender.

4. Stir in beans. Cover and cook on high heat setting 15 to 20 minutes or until slightly thickened.

1 Serving: Calories 335 (Calories from Fat 155); Fat 17g (Saturated 7g); Cholesterol 65mg; Sodium 820mg; Carbohydrate 24g (Dietary Fiber 6g); Protein 28g

% Daily Value: Vitamin A 18%; Vitamin C 20%; Calcium 6%; Iron 28%

Diet Exchanges: 1 Starch, 3 Medium-Fat Meat, 2 Vegetable

Chunky Pork and Beef Sausage Chili

▪ 6 servings ▪

SLOW COOKER:
3 1/2- to 6-quart

PREP TIME:
20 minutes

COOK TIME:
Low 8 to 10 hours
High 3 to 5 hours

Ingredient Substitution

For a "white" chili, leave out the sausage and use 2 pounds of pork. Add a can of great Northern or pinto beans instead of the black beans.

Serving Suggestion

Decided at the last minute to invite some friends over for chili? Stir in an extra can or two of your favorite beans. Each can will increase the number of servings by two.

Finishing Touch

Let everyone add his or her own special touch by passing bowls of shredded Cheddar cheese, chopped avocado, sliced jalapeño chilies, chopped onion, sliced ripe olives, chopped fresh cilantro and sour cream.

1 pound lean boneless pork, cut into 3/4-inch pieces

1/2 pound fully cooked smoked beef sausage, cut into 1/2-inch slices

1 large onion, chopped (1 cup)

2 medium stalks celery, sliced (1 cup)

2 cloves garlic, finely chopped

1 can (15 ounces) black beans, rinsed and drained

1 can (15 ounces) chunky tomato sauce

1 can (10 ounces) diced tomatoes and green chilies

1 cup water

1 1/2 teaspoons chili powder

1/2 teaspoon ground cumin

1/2 teaspoon salt

1/4 teaspoon pepper

1. Mix all ingredients in 3 1/2- to 6-quart slow cooker.

2. Cover and cook on low heat setting 8 to 10 hours (or high heat setting 3 to 5 hours) or until pork is tender.

1 Serving: Calories 380 (Calories from Fat 160); Fat 18g (Saturated 7g); Cholesterol 70mg; Sodium 1420mg; Carbohydrate 31g (Dietary Fiber 7g); Protein 30g

% Daily Value: Vitamin A 12%; Vitamin C 18%; Calcium 10%; Iron 22%

Diet Exchanges: 2 Starch, 3 Medium-Fat Meat

Meaty Main Dishes

◄ *Savory Pot Roast (page 59)*

Beef and Potatoes with Rosemary

▪ *8 servings* ▪

SLOW COOKER:
3 1/2- to 6-quart

PREP TIME:
20 minutes

COOK TIME:
Low 8 to 10 hours

Ingredient Substitution

Just run out of onions? You can add a teaspoon of onion powder with the mustard mixture to spread on the beef instead of chopping a fresh onion.

Finishing Touch

If your family likes gravy, you may want to thicken the beef juices. Skim fat from juices. Measure 1 1/2 cups of the juices from the cooker; pour into a small saucepan. Heat to boiling over medium-high heat. Shake 2 tablespoons cornstarch and 1/4 cup cold water in a tightly covered jar. Stir cornstarch mixture into beef juices. Cook about 5 minutes, stirring occasionally, until thickened.

1 pound medium red potatoes, cut into fourths

1 cup baby-cut carrots

3-pound beef boneless chuck roast

3 tablespoons Dijon mustard

2 tablespoons chopped fresh or 1 1/2 teaspoons dried rosemary leaves, crumbled

1 teaspoon chopped fresh or 1/2 teaspoon dried thyme leaves

1 teaspoon salt

1/2 teaspoon pepper

1 small onion, finely chopped (1/4 cup)

1 1/2 cups beef broth

1. Arrange potatoes and carrots in 3 1/2- to 6-quart slow cooker.

2. Trim excess fat from beef. Mix mustard, rosemary, thyme, salt and pepper; spread evenly over beef. Place beef in cooker. Sprinkle onion over beef. Pour broth evenly over beef and vegetables.

3. Cover and cook on low heat setting 8 to 10 hours or until beef and vegetables are tender.

4. Remove beef and vegetables from cooker, using slotted spoon; place on serving platter. Skim fat from beef juices in cooker if desired. Serve beef with juices.

1 Serving: Calories 250 (Calories from Fat 110); Fat 12g (Saturated 4g); Cholesterol 60mg; Sodium 550mg; Carbohydrate 14g (Dietary Fiber 2g); Protein 23g

% Daily Value: Vitamin A 24%; Vitamin C 6%; Calcium 2%; Iron 18%

Diet Exchanges: 1 Starch, 3 Lean Meat

Beef and Potatoes with Rosemary ➤

New England Pot Roast

■ 8 servings ■

SLOW COOKER:
4- to 6-quart

PREP TIME:
20 minutes

COOK TIME:
Low 8 to 10 hours

Betty's Success Tip

Yes, the entire jar of prepared horseradish is spread on top of the roast. The flavor of the horseradish becomes subtle during the long, slow cooking. It's our best kept secret ingredient we'd like to share with you! You can find horseradish in the refrigerator section of your supermarket.

Serving Suggestion

The great thing about serving a pot roast dinner is that everything—meat and vegetables—is included in one dish. Complete this easy meal with a good old-fashioned dessert, such as warm apple crisp, bread pudding or cherry cobbler.

3- to 3 1/2-pound beef boneless chuck roast

1 tablespoon vegetable oil

8 small potatoes, cut in half

3 cups baby-cut carrots

1 large onion, coarsely chopped (1 cup)

1 jar (5 ounces) prepared horseradish

1 teaspoon salt

1/2 teaspoon pepper

1 cup water

1. Trim excess fat from beef. Heat oil in 10-inch skillet over medium-high heat. Cook beef in oil about 10 minutes, turning occasionally, until brown on all sides.

2. Place potatoes, carrots and onions in 4- to 6-quart slow cooker. Place beef on vegetables. Mix horseradish, salt and pepper; spread evenly over beef.

3. Pour water over beef and vegetables. Cover and cook on low heat setting 8 to 10 hours or until beef and vegetables are tender.

1 Serving: Calories 345 (Calories from Fat 135); Fat 15g (Saturated 5g); Cholesterol 75mg; Sodium 390mg; Carbohydrate 30g (Dietary Fiber 4g); Protein 27g

% Daily Value: Vitamin A 70%; Vitamin C 16%; Calcium 4%; Iron 24%

Diet Exchanges: 1 Starch, 2 1/2 Medium-Fat Meat, 3 Vegetable

Savory Pot Roast

6 servings

SLOW COOKER:
4- to 6-quart

PREP TIME:
20 minutes

COOK TIME:
Low 8 to 10 hours

FINISHING COOK TIME:
High 15 minutes

Betty's Success Tip

A quick way to mix the flour with the liquid is to use a jar. Screw the lid on tight, and shake the jar until the mixture is smooth. This is faster than trying to stir it until all the lumps of flour are dissolved.

Ingredient Substitution

If you just have tomato juice in your cupboard, go ahead and use it instead of the eight-vegetable juice. Regular-size carrots, cut into 2-inch pieces, can be used if you are out of baby-cut carrots. And a drained 4-ounce can of sliced mushrooms can be used instead of the fresh mushrooms.

Serving Suggestion

Leftover beef and vegetable sauce? Turn it into savory beef and vegetable soup for another meal. Shred the beef, and stir it into the vegetable sauce. Add enough beef broth to make it the soup consistency that you like. Just heat it, and top each serving with a sprinkle of shredded Cheddar cheese. It's a great disguise for leftovers!

2- to 2 1/2-pound beef bottom round roast

2 teaspoons olive or vegetable oil

2 or 3 medium potatoes, cut into 2-inch pieces

2 1/2 cups baby-cut carrots

2 cups sliced mushrooms (about 5 ounces)

1 medium stalk celery, sliced (1/2 cup)

1 medium onion, chopped (1/2 cup)

1 teaspoon salt

1/2 teaspoon pepper

1/2 teaspoon dried thyme leaves

1 can (14 1/2 ounces) diced tomatoes, undrained

1 can (10 1/2 ounces) condensed beef consommé or broth

1 can (5 1/2 ounces) eight-vegetable juice

1/4 cup all-purpose flour

1. Trim excess fat from beef. Heat oil in 10-inch skillet over medium-high heat. Cook beef in oil about 10 minutes, turning occasionally, until brown on all sides.

2. Place potatoes, carrots, mushrooms, celery and onion in 4- to 6-quart slow cooker. Sprinkle with salt, pepper and thyme. Place beef on vegetables. Pour tomatoes, consommé and vegetable juice over beef.

3. Cover and cook on low heat setting 8 to 10 hours or until beef and vegetables are tender.

4. Remove beef and vegetables from cooker, using slotted spoon; place on serving platter and keep warm.

5. Skim fat from beef juices in cooker if desired. Remove 1/2 cup of the juices from the cooker; mix with flour until smooth. Gradually stir flour mixture into remaining juices in cooker. Cook on high heat setting about 15 minutes or until thickened. Serve sauce with beef and vegetables.

1 Serving: Calories 270 (Calories from Fat 55); Fat 6g (Saturated 2g); Cholesterol 75mg; Sodium 880mg; Carbohydrate 26g (Dietary Fiber 4g); Protein 32g

% Daily Value: Vitamin A 90%; Vitamin C 24%; Calcium 6%; Iron 26%

Diet Exchanges: 1 Starch, 3 Lean Meat, 2 Vegetable

Caramelized Onion Pot Roast

12 servings

Crowd SIZE

SLOW COOKER:
3 1/2- to 6-quart

PREP TIME:
25 minutes

COOK TIME:
Low 8 to 10 hours

What a Great Idea...
for Leftovers

If you're lucky enough to have leftovers from this flavor-packed roast, use them for making family-pleasing Easy Vegetable Beef Soup on page 62 or the 15-minute Quick Spaghetti Supper on page 63.

Chop the beef. Place 2 cups chopped beef in each freezer or refrigerator container. Add the onions and 1/4 cup beef juices to each container. Cover and refrigerate up to 4 days or freeze up to 4 months. To thaw frozen beef mixture, place container in the refrigerator about 8 hours.

4-pound beef boneless chuck roast

1 tablespoon olive or vegetable oil

1 teaspoon salt

1/2 teaspoon pepper

6 medium onions, sliced

1 1/2 cups beef broth

3/4 cup beer

2 tablespoons packed brown sugar

3 tablespoons Dijon mustard

2 tablespoons cider vinegar

1. Trim excess fat from beef. Heat oil in 10-inch skillet over medium-high heat. Cook beef in oil about 10 minutes, turning occasionally, until brown on all sides. Sprinkle with salt and pepper.

2. Place onions in 3 1/2- to 6-quart slow cooker. Place beef on onions.

3. Mix remaining ingredients; pour over beef and onions. Cover and cook on low heat setting 8 to 10 hours or until beef is tender.

4. Remove beef and onions from cooker, using slotted spoon. Cut beef into slices. Skim fat from beef juices in cooker if desired. Serve beef with juices.

1 Serving: Calories 205 (Calories from Fat 100); Fat 11g (Saturated 4g); Cholesterol 55mg; Sodium 420mg; Carbohydrate 8g (Dietary Fiber 1g); Protein 20g

% Daily Value: Vitamin A 0%; Vitamin C 2%; Calcium 2%; Iron 12%

Diet Exchanges: 2 Medium-Fat Meat, 2 Vegetable

what a
Great Idea...

Caramelized Onion Pot Roast ➤

...for Leftovers

What a Great Idea ... for Leftovers!

Supper will be on the table in just 20 minutes starting with a container of leftover Caramelized Onion Pot Roast (page 60). These two heartwarming recipes are short on time, but, oh so long on flavor.

Easy Vegetable-Beef Soup

PREP TIME: 5 minutes • COOK TIME: 15 minutes

■ *4 servings* ■

1 container (2 cups) Caramelized Onion Pot Roast (page 60), thawed if frozen

2 cups frozen mixed vegetables

1/4 cup uncooked quick-cooking barley

3 cups beef broth

1 teaspoon Dijon mustard

1. Mix all ingredients in 3-quart saucepan. Heat to boiling; reduce heat to low.

2. Cover and simmer about 12 minutes or until barley is tender.

1 Serving: Calories 300 (Calories from Fat 160); Fat 18g (Saturated 7g); Cholesterol 50mg; Sodium 900mg; Carbohydrate 18g (Dietary Fiber 4g); Protein 20g

% Daily Value: Vitamin A 16%; Vitamin C 14%; Calcium 4%; Iron 14%

Diet Exchanges: 1 Starch, 2 Medium-Fat Meat, 1 Vegetable, 1 Fat

Quick Spaghetti Supper

PREP TIME: 5 minutes • COOK TIME: 10 minutes

■ *4 servings* ■

1 container (2 cups) Caramelized
Onion Pot Roast (page 60),
thawed if frozen

1 jar (16 ounces) spaghetti sauce
(any flavor)

6 cups hot cooked spaghetti, for
serving

Grated Parmesan cheese, if desired

1. Heat roast mixture and spaghetti sauce in 3-quart saucepan over medium heat about 10 minutes, stirring occasionally, until hot.

2. Serve sauce over spaghetti. Sprinkle with cheese.

1 Serving: Calories 645 (Calories from Fat 210); Fat 23g (Saturated 7g); Cholesterol 50mg; Sodium 850mg; Carbohydrate 87g (Dietary Fiber 5g); Protein 27g

% Daily Value: Vitamin A 8%; Vitamin C 16%; Calcium 30%; Iron 0%

Diet Exchanges: 5 Starch, 1 High-Fat Meat, 2 Vegetable, 2 Fat

Brisket with Cranberry Gravy

■ *8 servings* ■

SLOW COOKER:
4- to 6-quart

PREP TIME:
10 minutes

COOK TIME:
Low 8 to 10 hours

2 1/2-pound fresh beef brisket (not corned beef)

1/2 teaspoon salt

1/4 teaspoon pepper

1 can (16 ounces) whole berry cranberry sauce

1 can (8 ounces) tomato sauce

1 medium onion, chopped (1/2 cup)

1 tablespoon mustard

1. Trim excess fat from beef. Rub surface of beef with salt and pepper. Place beef in 4- to 6-quart slow cooker. Mix remaining ingredients; pour over beef.

2. Cover and cook on low heat setting 8 to 10 hours or until beef is tender.

3. Cut beef across grain into thin slices. Skim fat from cranberry sauce in cooker if desired; serve with beef.

1 Serving: Calories 265 (Calories from Fat 70); Fat 8g (Saturated 3g); Cholesterol 60mg; Sodium 410mg; Carbohydrate 25g (Dietary Fiber 1g); Protein 24g

% Daily Value: Vitamin A 2%; Vitamin C 4%; Calcium 2%; Iron 12%

Diet Exchanges: 1 Starch, 2 1/2 Lean Meat, 2 Vegetable

Betty's Success Tip

Be sure to use a fresh beef brisket instead of a corned beef brisket. A "corned" brisket is a fresh brisket that has been cured in seasoned brine, which would overpower the delicate flavor of the cranberry gravy. If a fresh brisket isn't available, use the same cut of beef roast that you use for your favorite pot roast.

Ingredient Substitution

We like the appearance of the whole berry cranberry sauce, but you can use a can of jellied cranberries if you like. Cranberries are native to North America. Pilgrims noticed that cranes flew in great flocks to the cranberry bogs and feasted on the sour red berries. Thus the berries got the name "craneberries," which later became "cranberries."

Mexicali Round Steak

■ 6 servings ■

SLOW COOKER:
3 1/2- to 6-quart

PREP TIME:
15 minutes

COOK TIME:
Low 8 to 9 hours

Betty's Success Tip

Not everyone loves the assertive flavor of cilantro. When you cook cilantro for a long time, however, the flavor becomes very mild and blends into the overall flavor of the dish. When it is added at the end of cooking or used fresh, it can be the primary flavor. So give this recipe a try, and see whether the one who doesn't love cilantro even knows it's in the dish.

Ingredient Substitution

Vary the taste of this all-in-one meal by using pinto beans instead of the black beans and sprinkling with Cheddar cheese in place of the Monterey Jack cheese.

Finishing Touch

Serve with additional salsa to spoon on top of each serving, and sprinkle with additional chopped fresh cilantro. Pass a basket of warm tortillas to enjoy with this hearty steak meal.

1 1/2 pounds beef boneless round steak

1 cup frozen whole kernel corn, thawed

1 cup chopped fresh cilantro

1/2 cup beef broth

3 medium stalks celery, thinly sliced (1 1/2 cups)

1 large onion, sliced

1 jar (20 ounces) salsa

1 can (15 ounces) black beans, rinsed and drained

1 cup shredded Monterey Jack cheese with jalapeño peppers (4 ounces)

1. Trim excess fat from beef. Cut beef into 6 serving pieces. Place beef in 3 1/2- to 6-quart slow cooker. Mix remaining ingredients except cheese; pour over beef.

2. Cover and cook on low heat setting 8 to 9 hours or until beef is tender.

3. Sprinkle cheese over beef mixture.

1 Serving: Calories 320 (Calories from Fat 90); Fat 10g (Saturated 5g); Cholesterol 75mg; Sodium 760mg; Carbohydrate 32g (Dietary Fiber 8g); Protein 34g

% Daily Value: Vitamin A 14%; Vitamin C 20%; Calcium 24%; Iron 26%

Diet Exchanges: 1 Starch, 3 Lean Meat, 3 Vegetable

Swiss Steak Supper

■ 6 servings ■

SLOW COOKER:
3 1/2- to 6-quart

PREP TIME:
15 minutes

COOK TIME:
Low 7 to 9 hours

1 1/2 pounds beef boneless round steak

1/2 teaspoon peppered seasoned salt

6 to 8 new potatoes, cut into fourths

1 1/2 cups baby-cut carrots

1 medium onion, sliced

1 can (14 1/2 ounces) diced tomatoes with basil, garlic and oregano, undrained

1 jar (12 ounces) home-style beef gravy

Chopped fresh parsley, if desired

1. Trim excess fat from beef. Cut beef into 6 serving pieces. Spray 12-inch skillet with cooking spray; heat over medium-high heat. Sprinkle beef with seasoned salt. Cook beef in skillet about 8 minutes, turning once, until brown.

2. Layer potatoes, carrots, beef and onion in 3 1/2- to 6-quart slow cooker. Mix tomatoes and gravy; spoon over beef and vegetables.

3. Cover and cook on low heat setting 7 to 9 hours or until beef and vegetables are tender. Sprinkle with parsley.

1 Serving: Calories 230 (Calories from Fat 45); Fat 5g (Saturated 2g); Cholesterol 55mg; Sodium 590mg; Carbohydrate 24g (Dietary Fiber 3g); Protein 25g

% Daily Value: Vitamin A 50%; Vitamin C 16%; Calcium 4%; Iron 20%

Diet Exchanges: 1 Starch, 2 1/2 Very Lean Meat, 2 Vegetable

Betty's Success Tip

New potatoes are thin-skinned, small, young potatoes of any variety. They are waxy in texture because there hasn't been enough time for the sugar to convert to starch. Leaving the peel on the potatoes not only retains nutrients but also helps them to keep their shape during cooking.

Ingredient Substitution

Out of tomatoes with basil, garlic and oregano? Use a can of diced tomatoes, and add 1/2 teaspoon dried basil leaves, 1/4 teaspoon garlic powder and 1/2 teaspoon dried oregano leaves. And if you have only seasoned salt, use the same amount as the peppered seasoned salt and add 1/4 teaspoon black pepper.

Serving Suggestion

Eating enough servings of vegetables in one day is not always easy. This one-dish meal already has potatoes and carrots. Serve a green vegetable not only to add more color to your plate but also to provide half of your servings of vegetables for the day.

Hungarian Goulash

■ *8 servings* ■

SLOW COOKER:
3 1/2- to 6-quart

PREP TIME:
20 minutes

COOK TIME:
Low 8 to 10 hours
High 4 to 5 hours

FINISHING COOK TIME:
High 30 minutes

Ingredient Substitution

Just discovered you are all out of fresh garlic? Use 1/4 teaspoon garlic powder instead.

Finishing Touch

For a special touch, top each serving of goulash with a dollop of sour cream or toss the hot noodles with a tablespoon or two of poppy seed.

2 tablespoons vegetable oil

2 pounds beef stew meat, cut into 1-inch pieces

1 large onion, sliced

1 can (14 1/2 ounces) ready-to-serve beef broth

1 can (6 ounces) tomato paste

2 cloves garlic, finely chopped

1 tablespoon Worcestershire sauce

1 tablespoon paprika

1 teaspoon salt

1/4 teaspoon caraway seed, if desired

1/4 teaspoon pepper

1/4 cup cold water

3 tablespoons all-purpose flour

1 medium bell pepper, cut into strips

8 cups hot cooked noodles, for serving

1. Heat oil in 10-inch skillet over medium-high heat. Cook beef in oil about 10 minutes, stirring occasionally, until brown; drain. Place beef and onion in 3 1/2- to 6-quart slow cooker.

2. Mix broth, tomato paste, garlic, Worcestershire sauce, paprika, salt, caraway seed and pepper; stir into beef mixture.

3. Cover and cook on low heat setting 8 to 10 hours until beef is tender.

4. Mix water and flour; gradually stir into beef mixture. Stir in bell pepper. Cover and cook on high heat setting 30 minutes.

5. Serve goulash over noodles.

1 Serving: Calories 435 (Calories from Fat 135); Fat 15g (Saturated 5g); Cholesterol 110mg; Sodium 770mg; Carbohydrate 50g (Dietary Fiber 4g); Protein 29g

% Daily Value: Vitamin A 12%; Vitamin C 20%; Calcium 4%; Iron 32%

Diet Exchanges: 3 Starch, 2 1/2 Medium-Fat Meat, 1 Vegetable

Beef Stroganoff

■ 8 servings ■

SLOW COOKER:
3 1/2- to 6-quart

PREP TIME:
10 minutes

COOK TIME:
Low 8 to 10 hours

Betty's Success Tip

The soups not only add flavor but also provide a nice smooth creamy sauce for this stroganoff. The sour cream is stirred in at the end of cooking so it stays smooth and doesn't curdle the sauce.

Finishing Touch

Make this stroganoff extra special by replacing the canned mushrooms with sliced fresh mushrooms you add at the end of cooking. Sauté the mushrooms in a small amount of butter just until they brown. Stir mushrooms, and any remaining butter, in with the sour cream. Top off the stroganoff with a generous sprinkle of freshly chopped parsley.

2 pounds beef stew meat

1 large onion, chopped (1 cup)

1 can (10 3/4 ounces) condensed cream of golden mushroom soup

1 can (10 3/4 ounces) condensed cream of onion soup

1 can (8 ounces) sliced mushrooms, drained

1/4 teaspoon pepper

1 package (8 ounces) cream cheese, cubed

1 container (8 ounces) sour cream

6 cups hot cooked noodles or rice, for serving, if desired

1. Mix beef, onion, soups, mushrooms and pepper in 3 1/2- to 6-quart slow cooker.

2. Cover and cook on low heat setting 8 to 10 hours or until beef is very tender.

3. Stir cream cheese into beef mixture until melted. Stir in sour cream.

4. Serve beef mixture over noodles.

1 Serving: Calories 505 (Calories from Fat 325); Fat 36g (Saturated 17g); Cholesterol 145mg; Sodium 830mg; Carbohydrate 12g (Dietary Fiber 1g); Protein 34g

% Daily Value: Vitamin A 14%; Vitamin C 2%; Calcium 12%; Iron 22%

Diet Exchanges: 4 High-Fat Meat, 2 Vegetable, 1 Fat

Spinach-Stuffed Cubed Steaks

■ *4 servings* ■

SLOW COOKER:
2- to 3 1/2-quart

PREP TIME:
20 minutes

COOK TIME:
Low 8 to 9 hours

FINISHING COOK TIME:
10 minutes

Betty's Success Tip

Flatten the cubed steaks by placing them between sheets of plastic wrap or waxed paper and pounding with the flat side of a meat mallet or a rolling pin. Don't have a meat mallet or rolling pin? Press the heel of your hand over the top of the steak until it is evenly flattened.

Ingredient Substitution

Traditional pesto is a mixture of basil, garlic, olive oil and pine nuts. Today, however, this popular sauce can be made from other herbs and vegetables instead of basil. There is sun-dried tomato, roasted bell pepper and spinach pesto, just to mention a few, so use whichever pesto you like.

Finishing Touch

To add crunch and bright red color to this dish, add a chopped small red bell pepper to the sauce when you stir in the cornstarch mixture.

4 beef cubed steaks (about 1 1/4 pounds)

1/4 cup basil pesto

1 tablespoon plus 1 teaspoon instant minced onion

1 package (10 ounces) frozen chopped spinach, thawed and squeezed to drain

1/2 cup beef broth

1 teaspoon finely chopped garlic

1 tablespoon cornstarch

1 tablespoon water

1. Flatten each beef steak to 1/8-inch thickness. Spread 1 tablespoon pesto over each steak; sprinkle each with 1 teaspoon onion. Divide spinach among steaks, spreading to edges. Roll up steaks; secure with toothpicks.

2. Place steaks in 2- to 3 1/2-quart slow cooker. Mix broth and garlic; pour over steaks.

3. Cover and cook on low heat setting 8 to 9 hours or until beef is tender.

4. Remove steaks from cooker to serving platter; keep warm.

5. Skim fat from beef juices in cooker if desired. Measure 1 cup juices; pour into small saucepan. Mix cornstarch and water; stir into juices. Cook over medium-high heat about 5 minutes, stirring frequently, until thickened. Serve over steaks.

1 Serving: Calories 250 (Calories from Fat 110); Fat 12g (Saturated 3g); Cholesterol 75mg; Sodium 300mg; Carbohydrate 7g (Dietary Fiber 2g); Protein 31g

% Daily Value: Vitamin A 36%; Vitamin C 6%; Calcium 12%; Iron 20%

Diet Exchanges: 4 Lean Meat, 1 Vegetable

Picadillo

■ *12 servings* ■

Crowd
SIZE

SLOW COOKER:
3 1/2- to 6-quart

PREP TIME:
20 minutes

COOK TIME:
Low 3 to 4 hours

What a Great Idea. . . for Leftovers

This Mexican version of hash is great to have as a standby in the freezer. It adds a unique flavor twist to Picadillo Tacos (page 74) and Hash 'n Eggs (page 75). And use it as a filling the next time you make enchiladadas or tostadas.

Place 2 cups Picadillo in each freezer or refrigerator container. Cover and refrigerate up to 4 days or freeze up to 4 months. To thaw frozen Picadillo, place container in the refrigerator about 8 hours.

2 pounds ground beef

1 large onion, chopped (1 cup)

1 cup raisins

2 teaspoons chili powder

1 teaspoon salt

3/4 teaspoon ground cinnamon

1/2 teaspoon ground cumin

1/2 teaspoon pepper

2 cloves garlic, finely chopped

2 medium apples, peeled and chopped

2 cans (10 ounces each) diced tomatoes and green chilies, undrained

1/2 cup slivered almonds, toasted (page 152)

1. Cook beef and onion in 12-inch skillet over medium heat, stirring occasionally, until beef is brown; drain.

2. Mix beef mixture and remaining ingredients except almonds in 3 1/2- to 6-quart slow cooker.

3. Cover and cook on low heat setting 3 to 4 hours or until most of the liquid is absorbed. Stir in almonds.

1 Serving: Calories 245 (Calories from Fat 115); Fat 13g (Saturated 5g); Cholesterol 45mg; Sodium 310mg; Carbohydrate 18g (Dietary Fiber 2g); Protein 16g

% Daily Value: Vitamin A 4%; Vitamin C 8%; Calcium 4%; Iron 12%

Diet Exchanges: 2 Medium-Fat Meat, 1 Vegetable, 1 Fruit

what a Great Idea...

Picadillo ➤

...for Leftovers

What a Great Idea ... for Leftovers!

Picadillo (page 72) is made with a combination of ingredients that might surprise you—ground beef, apples, raisins, and almonds. The flavors and textures add a distinctive flair to these recipes.

Picadillo Tacos

PREP TIME: 5 minutes • COOK TIME: 5 minutes

■ *4 servings* ■

1 container (2 cups) Picadillo (page 72), thawed if frozen

8 taco shells

2 cups shredded lettuce

1 medium tomato, chopped (3/4 cup)

1 cup shredded Monterey Jack cheese (4 ounces)

1 cup sour cream

1. Heat Picadillo in small saucepan over medium heat about 5 minutes, stirring occasionally, until hot.

2. Fill taco shells with Picadillo. Top with remaining ingredients.

1 Serving: Calories 540 (Calories from Fat 325); Fat 36g (Saturated 17g); Cholesterol 95mg; Sodium 580mg; Carbohydrate 35g (Dietary Fiber 4g); Protein 23g

% Daily Value: Vitamin A 22%; Vitamin C 10%; Calcium 14%; Iron 34%

Diet Exchanges: 2 Starch, 2 Medium-Fat Meat, 1 Vegetable

Hash 'n Eggs

PREP TIME: 5 minutes • COOK TIME: 10 minutes

■ *4 servings* ■

1 container (2 cups) Picadillo
  (page 72), thawed if frozen

1 tablespoon margarine or butter

4 eggs

1/4 teaspoon salt

1/2 cup salsa

1/4 cup shredded Cheddar cheese
  (1 ounce)

1. Heat Picadillo in small saucepan over medium heat about 5 minutes, stirring occasionally, until hot.

2. Meanwhile, heat margarine in 10-inch skillet over medium heat. Crack eggs and slide each into skillet; reduce heat to low. Cook 3 minutes; sprinkle with salt. Turn eggs over; cook 1 to 2 minutes longer or until eggs are set.

3. Divide Picadillo among 4 plates. Top each with fried egg. Top with salsa; sprinkle with cheese.

1 Serving: Calories 330 (Calories from Fat 190); Fat 21g (Saturated 7g); Cholesterol 250mg; Sodium 650mg; Carbohydrate 17g (Dietary Fiber 2g); Protein 20g

% Daily Value: Vitamin A 16%; Vitamin C 10%; Calcium 10%; Iron 12%

Diet Exchanges: 1 Starch, 2 Medium-Fat Meat, 2 Fat

Cabbage Roll Casserole

■ 6 servings ■

SLOW COOKER:
3 1/2- to 6-quart

PREP TIME:
15 minutes

COOK TIME:
Low 4 to 6 hours

Betty's Success Tip

It is important to cook the ground beef before adding it to the cooker. Because the beef is ground, there is a greater risk that bacteria may start to grow before the temperature inside the cooker gets high enough.

Ingredient Substitution

No coleslaw mix on hand? Substitute 4 1/2 cups shredded cabbage and one shredded carrot. If you own a food processor with a shredding attachment, this is a great time to use it.

Finishing Touch

Place squares of process American cheese over the top of the finished casserole, or sprinkle with shredded Cheddar cheese. Cover and let it stand a few minutes so the cheese melts. Kids will love it!

1 pound ground beef

1 medium onion, chopped (1/2 cup)

5 cups coleslaw mix

1/2 cup uncooked instant rice

1/4 cup water

2 teaspoons paprika

1/2 teaspoon salt

1/4 teaspoon pepper

1 can (15 ounces) chunky Italian-style tomato sauce

1. Cook beef and onion in 10-inch skillet over medium heat, stirring occasionally, until beef is brown; drain.

2. Mix beef mixture and remaining ingredients in 3 1/2- to 6-quart slow cooker. (Cooker will be very full, but cabbage will cook down.)

3. Cover and cook on low heat setting 4 to 6 hours or until cabbage is tender.

1 Serving: Calories 300 (Calories from Fat 125); Fat 14g (Saturated 5g); Cholesterol 45mg; Sodium 600mg; Carbohydrate 27g (Dietary Fiber 3g); Protein 17g

% Daily Value: Vitamin A 24%; Vitamin C 28%; Calcium 6%; Iron 14%

Diet Exchanges: 1 Starch, 1 1/2 High-Fat Meat, 2 Vegetable

Veal Paprika

6 servings

SLOW COOKER:
3 1/2- to 6-quart

PREP TIME:
20 minutes

COOK TIME:
Low 6 to 8 hours

Betty's Success Tip

Paprika not only adds flavor to dishes but also adds color and a delightful aroma. The flavor of paprika can range from mild to pungent and hot, and the color can vary from orange-red to a very deep red. Most supermarkets carry only mild paprika, so you may want to check at an ethnic market for a more flavorful, hotter Hungarian paprika.

Ingredient Substitution

The flavor of paprika is also excellent with beef, so try this savory dish with beef stew meat.

Finishing Touch

Toss the noodles with poppy seed for a little crunch before serving with the veal mixture. To complement the flavor of the paprika, spoon a dollop of sour cream on top of each serving. A sprinkle of chopped fresh dill weed also adds a "fresh-flavor" lift to this dish.

3 tablespoons all-purpose flour

3/4 teaspoon salt

1 1/2 pounds veal stew meat

2 tablespoons vegetable oil

1 medium onion, chopped (1/2 cup)

1 can (8 ounces) tomato sauce

1 can (5 ounces) evaporated milk

2 tablespoons paprika

1 tablespoon Worcestershire sauce

6 cups hot cooked noodles, for serving

1. Mix flour and salt in resealable plastic bag. Add veal; shake until evenly coated. Heat oil in 10-inch skillet over medium heat. Cook veal in oil about 10 minutes, turning occasionally, until brown.

2. Mix veal and remaining ingredients except noodles in 3 1/2- to 6-quart slow cooker.

3. Cover and cook on low heat setting 6 to 8 hours or until veal is tender; stir.

4. Serve veal mixture over noodles.

1 Serving: Calories 395 (Calories from Fat 90); Fat 10g (Saturated 3g); Cholesterol 130mg; Sodium 650mg; Carbohydrate 51g (Dietary Fiber 3g); Protein 28g

% Daily Value: Vitamin A 20%; Vitamin C 6%; Calcium 12%; Iron 24%

Diet Exchanges: 3 Starch, 2 1/2 Lean Meat, 1 Vegetable

Braised Veal Shanks, Milan Style

■ *6 servings* ■

SLOW COOKER:
5- to 6-quart

PREP TIME:
30 minutes

COOK TIME:
Low 8 to 10 hours

Betty's Success Tip

Veal shanks are not always available, so check with your butcher to place an order ahead if necessary. You'll also find this succulent Milan masterpiece on restaurant menus under the name *ossobuco* or *ossibuchi*, which means "a hollowed bone."

Ingredient Substitution

If your family prefers beef to veal, go ahead and use beef shank cross cuts. Check with your butcher if you don't see them in the meat case.

Finishing Touch

This dish is often served with a refreshing condiment called *gremolata*. It is easy to make. Just mix 2 tablespoons chopped fresh parsley, a finely chopped clove of garlic and 1 teaspoon grated lemon peel. Pass the gremolata at the table to sprinkle on each serving.

4 pounds veal shanks

1/4 cup all-purpose flour

3 tablespoons olive or vegetable oil

1 medium onion, chopped (1/2 cup)

1 medium carrot, chopped (1/2 cup)

1 medium stalk celery, chopped (1/2 cup)

1 clove garlic, finely chopped

1/2 cup water

1/3 cup dry white wine

1 teaspoon salt

1/2 teaspoon dried basil leaves

1/2 teaspoon dried thyme leaves

1/4 teaspoon pepper

1. Trim excess fat from veal shanks. Coat veal with flour. Heat oil in 10-inch skillet over medium heat. Cook veal in oil about 20 minutes, turning occasionally, until brown on all sides; drain.

2. Place veal in 5- to 6-quart slow cooker. Mix remaining ingredients; pour over veal.

3. Cover and cook on low heat setting 8 to 10 hours or until veal is very tender and pulls away from bones.

4. Remove veal and vegetables from cooker, using slotted spoon; place on serving platter. Skim fat from veal juices in cooker if desired. Pour juices over veal and vegetables.

1 Serving: Calories 450 (Calories from Fat 180); Fat 20g (Saturated 6g); Cholesterol 255mg; Sodium 620mg; Carbohydrate 7g (Dietary Fiber 1g); Protein 62g

% Daily Value: Vitamin A 16%; Vitamin C 2%; Calcium 8%; Iron 18%

Diet Exchanges: 8 Lean Meat, 1 Vegetable

Braised Veal Shanks, Milan Style ➤

Pork Roast with Sherry-Plum Sauce

■ *12 servings* ■

SLOW COOKER:
3 1/2- to 6-quart

PREP TIME:
20 minutes

COOK TIME:
Low 7 to 9 hours

FINISHING COOK TIME:
High 15 minutes

What a Great Idea. . . for Leftovers

Too much roast for one meal? The leftover meal and sauce make handy "freezer buddies" for an easy Pork and Vegetable Stir-Fry (page 82) or Warm Cabbage, Apple and Pork Salad (page 83).

Cut pork into thin strips. Place 2 cups pork in each freezer or refrigerator container. Pour 1/4 cup sauce into each container. Cover and refrigerate up to 4 days or freeze up to 4 months. To thaw frozen pork mixture, place container in the refrigerator about 8 hours.

4-pound pork boneless loin roast

2 tablespoons vegetable oil

1 cup dry sherry

1 tablespoon ground mustard (dry)

2 tablespoons soy sauce

1 1/2 teaspoons dried thyme leaves

1 1/4 teaspoons ground ginger

1 teaspoon salt

1/4 teaspoon pepper

3 cloves garlic, finely chopped

1/2 cup plum jam

1. Trim excess fat from pork. Heat oil in 10-inch skillet over medium-high heat. Cook pork in oil about 10 minutes, turning occasionally, until brown on all sides.

2. Place pork in 3 1/2- to 6-quart slow cooker. Mix remaining ingredients except jam; pour over pork.

3. Cover and cook on low heat setting 7 to 9 hours or until pork is tender.

4. Remove pork from cooker; cover and keep warm. Skim fat from pork juices in cooker if desired. Stir jam into juices.

5. Cover and cook on high heat setting about 15 minutes or until jam is melted; stir. Serve sauce with pork.

1 Serving: Calories 240 (Calories from Fat 90); Fat 10g (Saturated 3g); Cholesterol 70mg; Sodium 400mg; Carbohydrate 12g (Dietary Fiber 0g); Protein 25g

% Daily Value: Vitamin A 0%; Vitamin C 0%; Calcium 0%; Iron 6%

Diet Exchanges: 1 Starch, 3 Lean Meat

what a Great Idea...

Pork Roast with Sherry-Plum Sauce ➤

for Leftovers ▶

What a Great Idea ... for Leftovers!

Pork Roast with Sherry-Plum Sauce (page 80) makes a great "keep on hand" leftover ready to add to your favorite Asian recipe. Below are two recipes using cooked pork that we found both quick and tasty.

Pork and Vegetable Stir-Fry

PREP TIME: 10 minutes • COOK TIME: 10 minutes

■ *4 servings* ■

1/4 cup apple juice

2 tablespoons dry sherry or apple juice

2 tablespoons soy sauce

1 tablespoon cornstarch

1 tablespoon vegetable oil

1/4 cup slivered almonds

1 package (16 ounces) fresh (refrigerated) stir-fry vegetables

1 clove garlic, finely chopped

1 container (2 cups) Pork Roast with Sherry-Plum Sauce (page 80), thawed if frozen

2 cups hot cooked rice, for serving

1. Shake apple juice or sherry, soy sauce and cornstarch in tightly covered container; set aside.

2. Heat oil in 12-inch skillet or wok over medium-high heat. Add almonds; stir-fry until golden brown. Remove almonds with slotted spoon; set aside.

3. Add stir-fry vegetables and garlic to skillet; cook about 5 minutes or until vegetables are crisp-tender.

4. Add pork mixture and juice mixture to skillet. Cook 2 to 3 minutes, stirring frequently, until sauce is thickened and bubbly.

5. Serve pork mixture over rice. Sprinkle with almonds.

1 Serving: Calories 305 (Calories from Fat 145); Fat 16g (Saturated 3g); Cholesterol 50mg; Sodium 930mg; Carbohydrate 22g (Dietary Fiber 5g); Protein 23g

% Daily Value: Vitamin A 36%; Vitamin C 32%; Calcium 6%; Iron 10%

Diet Exchanges: 1 Starch, 2 Medium-Fat Meat, 1 Vegetable, 1 Fat

Warm Cabbage, Apple and Pork Salad

PREP TIME: 20 minutes • COOK TIME: 10 minutes

■ *4 servings* ■

1 container (2 cups) Pork Roast with Sherry-Plum Sauce (page 80), thawed if frozen

Plum Dressing (below)

2 teaspoons vegetable oil

2 medium apples, cut into thin wedges

1 small onion, sliced

6 cups coleslaw mix or shredded cabbage

1/2 teaspoon salt

1/4 cup plum sauce reserved from pork

2 tablespoons plum jam

1 tablespoon cider vinegar

2 teaspoons Dijon mustard

1/4 teaspoon pepper

1. Drain plum sauce from pork mixture; reserve for Plum Dressing. Prepare Plum Dressing; set aside.

2. Heat oil in 12-skillet over medium heat. Cover and cook apples and onion in oil 5 minutes or until onion is tender. Stir in coleslaw mix; sprinkle with salt. Cover and cook about 2 minutes or until coleslaw is crisp-tender. Remove cabbage mixture from skillet; cover and keep warm.

3. Increase heat to medium-high. Cook pork in skillet about 2 minutes, stirring frequently, until warm. Stir in dressing. Cook about 1 minute or until slightly thickened.

4. Spoon pork mixture over cabbage mixture. Serve immediately.

Plum Dressing

Shake all ingredients in tightly covered container.

1 Serving: Calories 315 (Calories from Fat 90); Fat 90g (Saturated 3g); Cholesterol 50mg; Sodium 530mg; Carbohydrate 22g (Dietary Fiber 6g); Protein 21g

% Daily Value: Vitamin A 2%; Vitamin C 42%; Calcium 8%; Iron 10%

Diet Exchanges: 1 Starch, 2 Lean Meat, 2 Vegetable, 1 Fruit, 1/2 Fat

Garlic Pork Roast

■ *10 servings* ■

Crowd
SIZE

SLOW COOKER:
3 1/2- to 6-quart

PREP TIME:
20 minutes

COOK TIME:
Low 8 to 10 hours

What a Great Idea. . . for Leftovers

You'll want to make this roast to shred and pop in the freezer to have for those busy days. No one will know it took you less than 30 minutes to make Weeknight Pork Stew (page 86) or Spicy Pork Chili (page 87).

Remove pork from the cooking liquid; reserve the liquid. Cool pork slightly. Shred warm pork, using 2 forks. Place 2 cups shredded pork in each refrigerator or freezer container. Add 1/4 cup reserved cooking liquid to each container. Cover and refrigerate up to 4 days or freeze up to 4 months. To thaw frozen pork mixture, place container in the refrigerator about 8 hours.

3 1/2-pound pork boneless loin roast

1 tablespoon vegetable oil

1 teaspoon salt

1/2 teaspoon pepper

1 medium onion, sliced

3 cloves garlic, peeled

1 cup chicken broth or water

1. Trim excess fat from pork. Heat oil in 10-inch skillet over medium-high heat. Cook pork in oil about 10 minutes, turning occasionally, until brown on all sides. Sprinkle with salt and pepper.

2. Place onion and garlic in 3 1/2- to 6-quart slow cooker. Place pork on onion and garlic. Pour broth over pork.

3. Cover and cook on low heat setting 8 to 10 hours or until pork is tender.

1 Serving: Calories 200 (Calories from Fat 90); Fat 10g (Saturated 3g); Cholesterol 75mg; Sodium 280mg; Carbohydrate 2g (Dietary Fiber 0g); Protein 26g

% Daily Value: Vitamin A 0%; Vitamin C 0%; Calcium 0%; Iron 4%

Diet Exchanges: 4 Lean Meat

what a
Great Idea...

Garlic Pork Roast ➤

...for Leftovers

What a Great Idea ... for Leftovers!

Your family will quickly gather around the table when you serve these hearty dishes using leftover Garlic Pork Roast (page 84). No one can resist the subtle aroma of garlic when it fills the air!

Weeknight Pork Stew

PREP TIME: 10 minutes • COOK TIME: 20 minutes

■ *4 servings* ■

1 container (2 cups) Garlic Pork
  Roast (page 84), thawed if frozen

8 small new potatoes, cut into
  1/4-inch slices

2/3 cup vegetable, chicken or beef
  broth

1 1/4 teaspoons dried basil leaves

1/2 teaspoon salt

1 cup frozen green peas

2 teaspoons cornstarch

2 teaspoons water

1. Mix all ingredients except peas, cornstarch and water in 3-quart saucepan. Heat to boiling; reduce heat to low. Cover and simmer 10 to 12 minutes or until potatoes are tender.

2. Rinse peas with cold water to separate; stir into pork mixture. Cover and cook 2 minutes.

3. Mix cornstarch and water; stir into pork mixture. Cook and stir about 1 minute or until sauce is thickened.

1 Serving: Calories 220 (Calories from Fat 55); Fat 6g (Saturated 2g); Cholesterol 45mg; Sodium 670mg; Carbohydrate 27g (Dietary Fiber 4g); Protein 19g

% Daily Value: Vitamin A 4%; Vitamin C 12%; Calcium 2%; Iron 12%

Diet Exchanges: 1 Starch, 2 Lean Meat, 2 Vegetable

Spicy Pork Chili

PREP TIME: 5 minutes • COOK TIME: 15 minutes

■ *4 servings* ■

1 container (2 cups) Garlic Pork Roast (page 84), thawed if frozen

1 cup hot or medium salsa

1 to 2 teaspoons chili powder

1 can (15 or 16 ounces) pinto or kidney beans, rinsed and drained

1/2 cup shredded Colby-Monterey Jack cheese (2 ounces)

4 medium green onions, sliced (1/4 cup)

Sour cream, if desired

1. Mix all ingredients except cheese, onions and sour cream in 3-quart saucepan. Heat to boiling; reduce heat to low. Cover and simmer about 10 minutes or until hot.

2. Sprinkle each serving with cheese and onions. Top with sour cream.

1 Serving: Calories 300 (Calories from Fat 100); Fat 11g (Saturated 5g); Cholesterol 60mg; Sodium 610mg; Carbohydrate 32g (Dietary Fiber 11g); Protein 29g

% Daily Value: Vitamin A 10%; Vitamin C 14%; Calcium 16%; Iron 22%

Diet Exchanges: 2 Starch, 3 Lean Meat

what a Great Idea ...
Leftovers ➤

Pork Roast with Creamy Mustard Sauce

■ *8 servings* ■

SLOW COOKER:
3 1/2- to 6-quart

PREP TIME:
15 minutes

COOK TIME:
Low 7 to 9 hours

FINISHING COOK TIME:
High 15 minutes

Betty's Success Tip

To make quick work of chopping the vegetables, place them in a food processor and chop until fine.

Ingredient Substitution

White wine blends nicely with the flavor of mustard. If you don't have wine on hand, you can use chicken broth.

Serving Suggestion

Want to serve potatoes but tired of the same old boiled or baked potato? For a change, serve potato dumplings, German spaetzle or Italian gnocchi. The kids will think they're fun to eat. You will find them in the frozen section at the supermarket. Or look for a box of gnocchi in the dried pasta section of the store. Toss the cooked dumplings with melted butter, and add a sprinkle of chopped fresh parsley or dill weed for a touch of color and flavor.

2 1/2- to 3-pound pork boneless sirloin roast

1 tablespoon vegetable oil

3/4 cup dry white wine

2 tablespoons all-purpose flour

1 teaspoon salt

1/2 teaspoon pepper

2 medium carrots, finely chopped or shredded

1 medium onion, finely chopped (1/2 cup)

1 small shallot, finely chopped (2 tablespoons)

1/4 cup half-and-half

2 to 3 tablespoons country-style Dijon mustard

1. Trim excess fat from pork. Heat oil in 10-inch skillet over medium-high heat. Cook pork in oil about 10 minutes, turning occasionally, until brown on all sides.

2. Place pork in 3 1/2- to 6-quart slow cooker. Mix remaining ingredients except half-and-half and mustard; pour over pork.

3. Cover and cook on low heat setting 7 to 9 hours or until pork is tender.

4. Remove pork from cooker; cover and keep warm. Skim fat from pork juices in cooker if desired. Stir half-and-half and mustard into juices.

5. Cover and cook on high heat setting about 15 minutes or until slightly thickened. Serve sauce with pork.

1 Serving: Calories 175 (Calories from Fat 80); Fat 9g (Saturated 3g); Cholesterol 55mg; Sodium 390mg; Carbohydrate 5g (Dietary Fiber 1g); Protein 20g

% Daily Value: Vitamin A 24%; Vitamin C 2%; Calcium 2%; Iron 6%

Diet Exchanges: 2 1/2 Lean Meat, 1 Vegetable

Pork Chop Dinner with Apples and Squash

▪ 4 servings ▪

SLOW COOKER:
3 1/2- to 6-quart

PREP TIME:
20 minutes

COOK TIME:
Low 8 to 9 hours

Betty's Success Tip

You will want to use a variety of apple that will hold its shape rather than one that will become soft during cooking. Rome Beauty is a good choice. Also, the red color of its skin holds well, and some of the color will bleed into the flesh of the apple pieces during cooking to give it a rosy color.

Ingredient Substitution

Butternut squash resembles the shape of a light bulb or pear—wider at one end than the other. It usually weighs between 2 and 3 pounds and has a golden yellow to camel-colored shell. You also can use about 2 pounds of other winter squash, such as hubbard, buttercup or banana, cut into pieces.

Finishing Touch

Add a wonderful nutty flavor and crunch by sprinkling coarsely chopped toasted nuts over each serving. Try pecans, walnuts, hazelnuts or your favorite nut.

1 small butternut squash

3 large unpeeled cooking apples

4 pork loin chops, 3/4 inch thick (about 1 1/4 pounds)

3/4 cup sugar

2 tablespoons all-purpose flour

1 teaspoon ground cinnamon

1/2 teaspoon salt

1. Peel squash. Cut squash in half; remove seeds. Cut squash into 1/2-inch slices. Cut apples into fourths; remove cores. Cut apple pieces crosswise in half. Remove excess fat from pork.

2. Layer squash and apples in 3 1/2- to 6-quart slow cooker. Mix remaining ingredients. Coat pork with sugar mixture. Place pork on apples. Sprinkle with any remaining sugar mixture.

3. Cover and cook on low heat setting 8 to 9 hours or until pork is tender.

1 Serving: Calories 440 (Calories from Fat 80); Fat 9g (Saturated 3g); Cholesterol 65mg; Sodium 340mg; Carbohydrate 71g (Dietary Fiber 5g); Protein 24g

% Daily Value: Vitamin A 38%; Vitamin C 14%; Calcium 4%; Iron 10%

Diet Exchanges: 2 Starch, 2 Lean Meat, 2 Vegetable, 2 Fruit

Pork Chops with Mixed Dried Fruit

■ 4 servings ■

SLOW COOKER:
3 1/2- or 6-quart

PREP TIME:
15 minutes

COOK TIME:
Low 6 to 7 hours

FINISHING COOK TIME:
High 6 minutes

4 pork loin chops, about 3/4 inch thick (about 1 1/4 pounds)

1 package (8 ounces) mixed dried fruit (1 1/2 cups)

3 tablespoons packed brown sugar

3 tablespoons orange marmalade

2 tablespoons cider vinegar

1/2 teaspoon ground ginger

1 can (5 1/2 ounces) apricot nectar

1 tablespoon cornstarch

2 tablespoons water

1. Place pork in 3 1/2- or 6-quart slow cooker. Layer dried fruit evenly over pork. Mix brown sugar, marmalade, vinegar, ginger and nectar; pour over pork and fruit.

2. Cover and cook on low heat setting 6 to 7 hours or until pork is slightly pink when cut near bone.

3. Remove pork and fruit from cooker, using slotted spoon; cover and keep warm.

4. Skim fat from pork juices in cooker if desired. Pour juices into 1-quart saucepan. Mix cornstarch and water; stir into juices. Cook on high heat 4 to 6 minutes, stirring constantly, until thickened and bubbly. Serve sauce with pork and fruit.

1 Serving: Calories 395 (Calories from Fat 70); Fat 8g (Saturated 3g); Cholesterol 65mg; Sodium 60mg; Carbohydrate 61g (Dietary Fiber 4g); Protein 24g

% Daily Value: Vitamin A 18%; Vitamin C 2%; Calcium 4%; Iron 14%

Diet Exchanges: 2 Starch, 2 1/2 Lean Meat, 2 Fruit

Betty's Success Tip

Check that the package of dried fruit contains large pieces of fruit, such as slices of peaches, apples, pears and apricots. Diced dried fruit is also available, but the pieces are so small that they overcook and become part of the sauce during the long, slow cooking.

Ingredient Substitution

Although apricot nectar enhances the flavors of the dried fruit, feel free to also use 3/4 cup of another light-colored fruit juice, such as apple, orange or pineapple.

Serving Suggestion

Parsley-buttered new potatoes and steamed baby carrots are all that is needed to complete this Scandinavian-influenced dish and satisfy everyone at dinner.

Smoky-Flavored Barbecued Ribs

■ 4 servings ■

Slow Cooker:
5- to 6-quart

Prep Time:
15 minutes

Cook Time:
Low 8 to 9 hours

Finishing Cook Time:
Low 1 hour

3 1/2 pounds pork loin back ribs

1/4 cup packed brown sugar

1/2 teaspoon pepper

3 tablespoons liquid smoke

2 cloves garlic, finely chopped

1 teaspoon salt

1 medium onion, sliced

1/2 cup cola

1 1/2 cups barbecue sauce

1. Spray inside of 5- to 6-quart slow cooker with cooking spray.

2. Remove inner skin from ribs. Mix brown sugar, pepper, liquid smoke, garlic and salt; rub mixture into ribs. Cut ribs into about 4-inch pieces. Layer ribs and onion in slow cooker. Pour cola over ribs.

3. Cover and cook on low heat setting 8 to 9 hours or until ribs are tender. Remove ribs from cooker. Drain liquid from cooker and discard.

4. Pour barbecue sauce into shallow bowl. Dip ribs into sauce. Place ribs in cooker. Pour any remaining sauce over ribs. Cover and cook on low heat setting 1 hour.

Ingredient Substitution

Cola adds a wonderful sweetness to the ribs, but you can use water instead if you don't have any cola on hand. Pork ribs are by far the most popular choice for barbecued ribs, but try beef short ribs for a change. Trim any excess fat from the short ribs before adding them to the cooker.

Serving Suggestion

Busy day? Stop at the deli and pick up some potato salad and baked beans for an easy, old-fashioned southern barbecued rib dinner.

1 Serving: Calories 890 (Calories from Fat 540); Fat 60g (Saturated 22g); Cholesterol 230mg; Sodium 1540mg; Carbohydrate 32g (Dietary Fiber 2g); Protein 58g

% Daily Value: Vitamin A 8%; Vitamin C 6%; Calcium 12%; Iron 26%

Diet Exchanges: 2 Starch, 7 High-Fat Meat

Smoky-Flavored Barbecued Ribs ➤

Scalloped Potato and Sausage Supper

▪ *4 servings* ▪

SLOW COOKER:
3 1/2- to 6-quart

PREP TIME:
10 minutes

COOK TIME:
Low 4 to 5 hours

FINISHING COOK TIME:
Low 5 minutes

Betty's Success Tip

If you are watching the sodium and fat in your diet, use reduced-fat sausage and reduced-sodium soup in this all-family favorite.

Ingredient Substitution

Check your cupboard and discover that you have other cans of cream soup but not cream of mushroom with garlic? Use one of the other cream soups, and add 1/4 teaspoon of garlic powder.

Serving Suggestion

This dish makes a great family dinner on a busy fall evening. Add a crisp green tossed salad and some long, thin, crunchy breadsticks.

1 package (5 ounces) scalloped potato mix

1 can (10 3/4 ounces) condensed cream of mushroom with garlic soup

1 soup can water

1 pound fully cooked kielbasa sausage, cut into 2-inch diagonal pieces

1 cup frozen green peas

1. Spray 3 1/2- to 6-quart slow cooker with cooking spray. Place uncooked potatoes in slow cooker. Mix soup, water and Sauce Mix (from potato mix); pour over potatoes. Top with sausage.

2. Cover and cook on low heat setting 4 to 5 hours or until potatoes are tender.

3. Rinse peas with cold water to separate. Sprinkle peas over potatoes. Cover and cook on low heat setting about 5 minutes or until peas are hot.

1 Serving: Calories 400 (Calories from Fat 305); Fat 34g (Saturated 12g); Cholesterol 65mg; Sodium 1460mg; Carbohydrate 10g (Dietary Fiber 2g); Protein 16g

% Daily Value: Vitamin A 2%; Vitamin C 2%; Calcium 4%; Iron 10%

Diet Exchanges: 2 High-Fat Meat, 2 Vegetable, 3 Fat

Lamb Dijon

■ 6 servings ■

SLOW COOKER:
3 1/2- to 6-quart

PREP TIME:
25 minutes

COOK TIME:
Low 8 to 10 hours
High 4 to 5 hours

FINISHING COOK TIME:
High 15 minutes

Betty's Success Tip

Grate the lemon peel before squeezing the lemon for juice, being careful to grate only the yellow part of the peel because the white pith is very bitter. To get the most juice from a lemon, roll it on a counter while pushing down firmly to break the tissues inside, which will release the juice. Or heat the lemon in the microwave for a minute, which also helps to release the juice.

Ingredient Substitution

For a Dijon-flavored beef dish, use the same amount of beef stew meat instead of lamb.

Finishing Touch

Gremolata, which is served with Italian braised veal shanks, would also be yummy sprinkled over this lamb dish. Just mix 2 tablespoons chopped fresh parsley, a finely chopped clove of garlic and 1 teaspoon grated lemon peel. Sprinkle it over each serving of lamb.

1/4 cup all-purpose flour

1 teaspoon salt

1/4 teaspoon pepper

2 tablespoons vegetable oil

2 pounds lamb stew meat

6 new potatoes (1 1/4 pounds), cubed

1/4 cup Dijon mustard

1/2 teaspoon grated lemon peel

1 tablespoon lemon juice

2 teaspoons chopped fresh or 1/2 teaspoon dried rosemary leaves

2 cloves garlic, finely chopped

1 can (14 1/2 ounces) ready-to-serve beef broth

1 package (10 ounces) frozen green peas, thawed

1. Mix flour, salt and pepper in resealable plastic bag. Add lamb; shake until evenly coated. Heat oil in 12-inch skillet over medium-high heat. Cook lamb in oil about 20 minutes, stirring occasionally, until brown; drain.

2. Mix lamb and remaining ingredients except peas in 3 1/2- to 6-quart slow cooker.

3. Cover and cook on low heat setting 8 to 10 hours or until lamb is tender.

4. Skim fat from juices in cooker. Stir peas into lamb mixture.

5. Cover and cook on high heat setting 10 to 15 minutes or until peas are hot.

1 Serving: Calories 300 (Calories from Fat 90); Fat 10g (Saturated 3g); Cholesterol 85mg; Sodium 940mg; Carbohydrate 30g (Dietary Fiber 5g); Protein 32g

% Daily Value: Vitamin A 2%; Vitamin C 12%; Calcium 4%; Iron 24%

Diet Exchanges: 2 Starch, 3 1/2 Lean Meat

Barbecue Beef Sandwiches

■ *12 sandwiches* ■

SLOW COOKER:
4- to 5-quart

PREP TIME:
20 minutes

COOK TIME:
Low 7 to 8 hours

FINISHING COOK TIME:
Low 30 minutes

Ingredient Substitution

If you don't have apricot pre-serves, you certainly may use peach preserves or orange mar-malade in its place.

Finishing Touch

For a delicious kick, spread buns with horseradish sauce. Sand-wiches can be served au jus. Serve the juices left in the cooker in small bowls to dip the sandwiches in while eating to make each bite extra delicious!

3-pound beef boneless chuck roast

1 cup barbecue sauce

1/2 cup apricot preserves

1/3 cup chopped green bell pepper

1 tablespoon Dijon mustard

2 teaspoons packed brown sugar

1 small onion, sliced

12 kaiser or hamburger buns, split

1. Trim excess fat from beef. Cut beef into 4 pieces. Place beef in 4- to 5-quart slow cooker.

2. Mix remaining ingredients except buns; pour over beef. Cover and cook on low heat setting 7 to 8 hours or until beef is tender.

3. Remove beef to cutting board; cut into thin slices; return to cooker.

4. Cover and cook on low heat setting 20 to 30 minutes longer or until beef is hot. Fill buns with beef mixture.

1 Sandwich: Calories 410 (Calories from Fat 145); Fat 16g (Saturated 5g); Cholesterol 70mg; Sodium 520mg; Carbohydrate 39g (Dietary Fiber 2g); Protein 29g

% Daily Value: Vitamin A 4%; Vitamin C 8%; Calcium 6%; Iron 24%

Diet Exchanges: 2 1/2 Starch, 3 Medium-fat Meat

Barbecue Beef Sandwich ➤

12 BROWN PAPER GOODS

Italian Beef and Green Pepper Sandwiches

■ 6 sandwiches ■

SLOW COOKER:
3 1/2- to 6-quart

PREP TIME:
15 minutes

COOK TIME:
Low 8 to 10 hours

FINISHING COOK TIME:
High 15 minutes

Betty's Success Tip

Brisket is an excellent cut to prepare in the slow cooker because
the long, slow cooking ensures
tenderness. Use this recipe as a
guideline for preparing your
favorite brisket recipe.

Ingredient Substitution

If you don't have crushed red pepper, just add a few drops of red
pepper sauce when you return the
beef slices to the cooker.

Finishing Touch

Sprinkle shredded mozzarella
cheese and sliced ripe olives over
the top of each sandwich.

2-pound fresh beef brisket

1 tablespoon vegetable oil

1 can (10 1/2 ounces) condensed beef broth

2 cloves garlic, finely chopped

1 teaspoon dried oregano leaves

1 teaspoon dried basil leaves

1/2 teaspoon salt

1/4 teaspoon pepper

1/4 teaspoon crushed red pepper

2 medium green bell peppers, cut into 1/4-inch strips

12 slices crusty Italian or French bread, each about 1 inch thick

1. Trim excess fat from beef. Heat oil in 10-inch skillet over medium-high heat. Cook beef in oil about 10 minutes, turning occasionally, until both sides are brown.

2. Place beef in 3 1/2- to 6-quart slow cooker. Mix remaining ingredients except bell peppers and bread; pour over beef.

3. Cover and cook on low heat setting 8 to 10 hours or until beef is tender.

4. Remove beef to cutting board; cut into thin slices.

5. Skim fat from beef juices in cooker if desired. Stir bell peppers into juices. Cover and cook on high heat setting 15 minutes. Return beef slices to cooker.

6. Place 2 slices of bread on each plate. Spoon beef mixture over bread.

1 Sandwich: Calories 300 (Calories from Fat 100); Fat 11g (Saturated 4g); Cholesterol 65mg; Sodium 720mg; Carbohydrate 23g (Dietary Fiber 2g); Protein 29g

% Daily Value: Vitamin A 2%; Vitamin C 30%; Calcium 4%; Iron 20%

Diet Exchanges: 1 Starch, 3 Lean Meat, 2 Vegetable

Sloppy Joes

■ *24 sandwiches* ■

Slow Cooker:
3 1/2- to 6-quart

Prep Time:
15 minutes

Cook Time:
Low 7 to 9 hours
High 3 to 4 hours

Betty's Success Tip

Next time you're asked to bring something to one of your kid's events, bring Sloppy Joes. Kids love them. And you can keep the sandwich filling warm in the cooker for a couple of hours. Just be sure to stir it occasionally so that it doesn't start to get too brown around the edges.

Ingredient Substitution

Stir 1 cup drained sauerkraut into the mixture before serving. It will add a nice flavor twist, and no one will guess the "secret ingredient."

Serving Suggestion

You can serve this tasty beef mixture over hot cooked rice or pasta rather than using as a sandwich filling. Or spoon it over tortilla chips and top each serving with shredded lettuce and shredded cheese.

3 pounds ground beef

1 large onion, coarsely chopped (1 cup)

3/4 cup chopped celery

1 cup barbecue sauce

1 can (26 1/2 ounces) sloppy joe sauce

24 hamburger buns

1. Cook beef and onion in Dutch oven over medium heat, stirring occasionally, until beef is brown; drain.

2. Mix beef mixture and remaining ingredients except buns in 3 1/2- to 6-quart slow cooker.

3. Cover and cook on low heat setting 7 to 9 hours (or high heat setting 3 to 4 hours) or until vegetables are tender.

4. Uncover and cook on high heat setting until desired consistency. Stir well before serving. Fill buns with beef mixture.

1 Sandwich: Calories 155 (Calories from Fat 80); Fat 9g (Saturated 3g); Cholesterol 30mg; Sodium 270mg; Carbohydrate 8g (Dietary Fiber 1g); Protein 11g

% Daily Value: Vitamin A 2%; Vitamin C 4%; Calcium 2%; Iron 6%

Diet Exchanges: 1 High-Fat Meat, 2 Vegetable

Ginger-Orange Beef Pita Sandwiches

■ *6 sandwiches* ■

Slow Cooker:
3 1/2- to 6-quart

Prep Time:
25 minutes

Cook Time:
Low 4 to 6 hours

Finishing Cook Time:
Low 15 minutes

Betty's Success Tip

To peel or not to peel ginger-root—that is the question. The great thing is, you can do either! Plus, if you would rather not spend the extra couple of minutes finely chopping the gingerroot, use a grater instead. Grate against the fibrous strings on the narrow ends of the gingerroot instead of the wider flat side. You can also see the fibers when you slice off a piece of gingerroot.

Serving Suggestion

This gingery beef mixture makes a fabulous sandwich, and it also makes a fabulous dinner when served with hot cooked basmati or jasmine rice and chutney. Finish the dinner with a cup of steaming tea and a bowl of coconut pudding.

1 pound beef boneless round steak

1 medium red onion, cut into eighths

1 medium orange bell pepper, cut into 1-inch pieces (1 1/2 cups)

1 medium jicama, peeled and cut into julienne strips (1 1/2 cups)

1 tablespoon grated orange peel

1/3 cup orange juice

1 teaspoon finely chopped gingerroot

1/2 teaspoon salt

1 package (6 ounces) frozen snap pea pods, thawed

3 pita breads (6 inches in diameter), cut in half to form pockets

Golden Fruit Chutney (page 177) or other chutney, if desired

1. Trim excess fat from beef. Cut beef lengthwise into 2-inch strips. Cut strips crosswise into 1/8-inch slices.

2. Place beef, onion, bell pepper and jicama in 3 1/2- to 6-quart slow cooker. Mix orange peel, orange juice, gingerroot and salt; pour over beef and vegetables.

3. Cover and cook on low heat setting 4 to 6 hours or until beef is tender.

4. Stir in snap pea pods. Cover and cook on low heat setting about 15 minutes or until pea pods are crisp-tender.

5. Spoon beef mixture into pita breads. Serve with Golden Fruit Chutney.

1 Sandwich: Calories 195 (Calories from Fat 25); Fat 3g (Saturated 1g); Cholesterol 35mg; Sodium 370mg; Carbohydrate 31g (Dietary Fiber 7g); Protein 18g

% Daily Value: Vitamin A 2%; Vitamin C 80%; Calcium 6%; Iron 18%

Diet Exchanges: 2 1/2 Very Lean Meat, 2 Fruit

Bratwurst and Sauerkraut

■ 6 sandwiches ■

SLOW COOKER:
3 1/2- to 6-quart

PREP TIME:
5 minutes

COOK TIME:
Low 4 to 5 hours

4 fully cooked bratwurst (about 4 ounces each), cut into 1/2-inch slices

2 cans (14 1/2 ounces each) sauerkraut, drained

1/3 cup packed brown sugar

6 hot dog or bratwurst buns

1. Mix all ingredients except buns in 3 1/2- to 6-quart slow cooker.

2. Cover and cook on low heat setting 4 to 5 hours.

3. Fill buns with bratwurst mixture.

1 Sandwich: Calories 450 (Calories from Fat 215); Fat 24g (Saturated 8g); Cholesterol 45mg; Sodium 2090mg; Carbohydrate 48g (Dietary Fiber 5g); Protein 15g

% Daily Value: Vitamin A 0%; Vitamin C 18%; Calcium 14%; Iron 26%

Diet Exchanges: 2 Starch, 1 High-Fat Meat, 3 Vegetable, 3 Fat

Betty's Success Tip

Check that the brats you buy are fully cooked rather than fresh. The juice that would be released from fresh brats during cooking would add too much liquid to the mixture. If you find sauerkraut to be too salty, rinse it in a strainer under cold water to remove some of the saltiness.

Ingredient Substitution

To add that something special to this dish, stir in 1/4 teaspoon caraway seed with the other ingredients. The spicy, aromatic seed comes from an herb of the parsley family.

Finishing Touch

Chopped raw onions are good with sauerkraut and brats, so be sure there is plenty ready to spoon into this sandwich. And remember to pass the mustard—either the All-American yellow mustard or a spicier coarse-ground one.

Sweet and Saucy Ham Sandwiches

■ *12 sandwiches* ■

SLOW COOKER:
3 1/2- to 6-quart

PREP TIME:
15 minutes

COOK TIME:
Low 3 to 4 hours

FINISHING COOK TIME:
High 15 minutes

1 1/2 pounds fully cooked smoked ham, ground (4 cups)

1 cup packed brown sugar

1/2 cup Dijon mustard

1/4 cup chopped green bell pepper

1 tablespoon instant minced onion

1 can (20 ounces) crushed pineapple in juice, undrained

12 hamburger buns

1. Mix all ingredients except buns in 3 1/2- to 6-quart slow cooker.

2. Cover and cook on low heat setting 3 to 4 hours.

3. Uncover and cook on high heat setting about 15 minutes or until desired consistency. Stir well before serving. Fill buns with ham mixture.

1 Sandwich: Calories 325 (Calories from Fat 70); Fat 8g (Saturated 2g); Cholesterol 35mg; Sodium 1230mg; Carbohydrate 48g (Dietary Fiber 2g); Protein 17g

% Daily Value: Vitamin A 0%; Vitamin C 4%; Calcium 10%; Iron 16%

Diet Exchanges: 1 Starch, 2 Lean Meat, 1 Vegetable, 2 Fruit

Betty's Success Tip

If you have a food processor, use it to finely chop the ham instead of grinding it. Or to save time, ask your butcher to grind it for you.

Ingredient Substitution

You can use your kids' favorite—bologna—instead of the ham. Find a 1 1/2-pound piece at the deli. If you don't have any instant minced onion on your spice rack, use 1/4 cup finely chopped onion.

Serving Suggestion

Complement the sweet-and-sour flavor of this ham filling by serving fresh fruit with the sandwiches. Arrange big, juicy red strawberries, cubes or balls of honeydew melon and cantaloupe, papaya slices and chunks of pineapple on a platter. Tuck a bowl of toasted coconut in the center of the platter to sprinkle on the fruit.

Adjustable Wrench

Another common wrench that you may actually have used, the adjustable wrench has one fixed, and one adjustable jaw. The jaws are designed to work against flat surfaces, such as a plumbing nut. The adjustable jaw allows the wrench to work with a large variety of nut sizes.

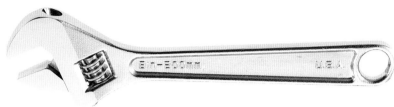

Slip Joint Pliers

Also know as tongue-and-groove or channel lock pliers, these pliers work much like the adjustable wrench above, but the jaws "lock" to specific opening sizes. The jaws often have a toothed rounded inner surface to allow work with both cylindrical pipes and flat-surfaced nuts, making it a very versatile tool.

PTFE (Teflon) Tape

Polytetrafluoroethylene tape, or more commonly referred to as Teflon tape, is used to make threaded plumbing joints watertight. The thin tape is wrapped around the threads on the pipe, and as the nut is tightened the tape is forced into the threads adding a pliable and reliable water seal.

Propane Torch

A reasonably safe and easily adjustable source of high heat, the propane torch is used to solder plumbing fittings. Used with flux and solder, the torch is fed by propane gas and the nozzle is re-used. A steel striking tool is used to ignite the torch, though many nozzles available today offer an integral ignition device. While an indispensable plumbing tool, caution should be used and practice is recommended.

SECTION ONE

Basics

Four Ways to Cut Steel or Iron Pipe

WHEN YOU'RE RUNNING PLUMBING, YOUR GOING TO NEED TO MAKE YOUR PIPES FIT. THE FIRST STEP IS CUTTING THEM TO LENGTH.

While there are flexible pipe options available in plumbing, much plumbing still relies on copper and iron pipe. Getting it cut to the proper length makes the job much easier.

1 Step one is to clamp the pipe in a vise ...

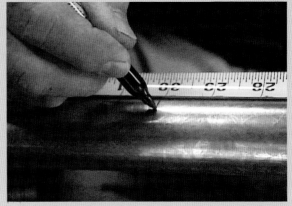

2 ... then measure and mark it to length.

3 A heavy duty pipe cutter is the first tool I'll show you.

4 It fits around the pipe, and then the handle is turned to just tighten against the pipe. One revolution on the handle, and then the cutter is spun around the outside of the pipe, riding on the guide roller.

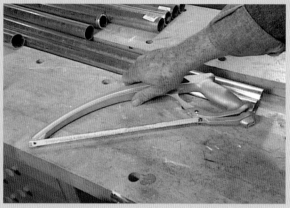

5 Another revolution on the handle, and another spin around the pipe. This action is repeated until the pipe separates cleanly.

6 A hacksaw with a blade that has eighteen or twenty-four teeth per inch will also do the trick.

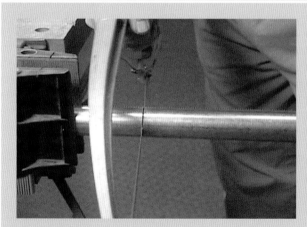

7 But you will get a fairly vigorous upper body workout.

8 As the saw exits the pipe, a slower stroke will leave a cleaner edge on the pipe.

9 This cordless portable band saw does the same job in a mere fraction of the time.

10 But you will miss out on the aerobic workout.

11 One more option is a metal cutoff saw like this one that uses an abrasive blade.

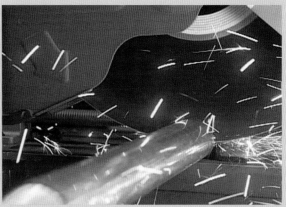

12 It's as quick as slicing salami, but be sure and wear a face shield, because it produces an impressive fireworks display to boot.

Connecting Copper Pipes

JOINING COPPER WATER SUPPLY LINES IS AN ART FORM, BUT THE STEPS ARE ACTUALLY FAIRLY SIMPLE.

With only a few simple tools and a little practice, you'll be sweating pipes like the pros.

1 With my pipes cut to the necessary length, I sand the ends to remove any surface dirt and oxidation using a plumber's emery cloth. A light sanding with a piece of fine-grit sandpaper is perfect.

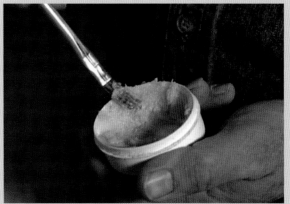

2 With the pipe clean, I next apply soldering flux.

3 This paste helps the solder flow evenly and promotes a good bond between the solder and the metal.

4 The inside of the fittings also need cleaning and this I do with a wire brush made just for this purpose.

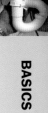

5 Once I finish the cleaning, I coat the inside of the fitting with the flux. Now I can slip the pieces together.

6 The copper is heated with a torch. Tool of choice is a propane torch. The one shown here uses a torch lighter to provide the spark. Others on the market have a built-in ignition system, much like your grill.

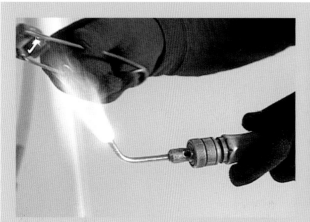

7 Once the torch is lit, the flame is adjusted to provide a blue flame that presents a cone-shape in the center of the flame. This will provide the optimal heat for heating the pipes.

8 The flame is played around the joined areas of the pipe for a short while (ten to twenty seconds is usually enough).

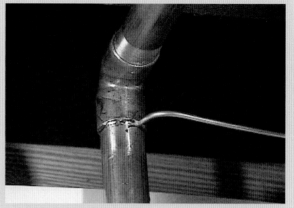

9 When the pipe and fitting reach the correct temperature, the tip of the solder is touched to the metal.

10 The solder melts instantly and is drawn into the joint by capillary action.

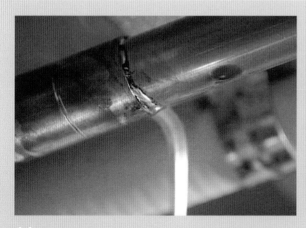

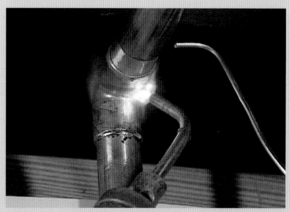

11 Notice how the solder is bent into an L-shape to more easily reach around the pipe.

12 In most cases a two- or three-part joint can be heated as one and the solder applied to all joints at the same time, but the joints can be heated and soldered one-at-a-time as well. Be careful of dripping solder as it is extremely hot.

Connecting PVC Pipes

VERSATILE AND EASY TO WORK WITH, PVC PIPING IS A STAPLE IN HOME PLUMBING

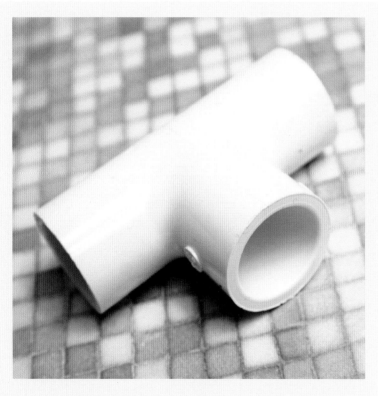

Much like Tinker Toys, linking PVC (polyvinyl chloride) pipes together can be fun. A little cement adds a permanent, water-proof seal.

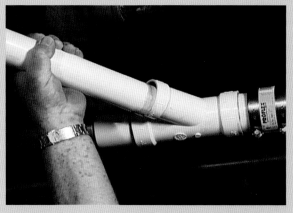

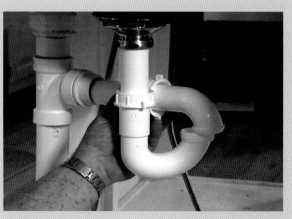

1 Cutting PVC pipe is easy. A fine-tooth saw adequate for most woodworking tasks will work fine here, as well.

2 PVC offers a wide variety of pre-formed connections and angles that make the process more of a puzzle than a chore.

3 Most plumbing fittings quickly attach to PVC piping with compression fittings. This makes them easy to assemble without any glues, and it also leaves the joint easy to disassemble ... just in case.

4 Many under-sink PVC connections are screw-together compression joints as well.

5 I first apply a purple primer ...

6 ... to both the fitting and the pipe ...

7 ... followed by an application of PVC cement.

8 A good rule of thumb when applying the primer and cement is to make three rotations around the outside of the pipe or the inside of the fitting.

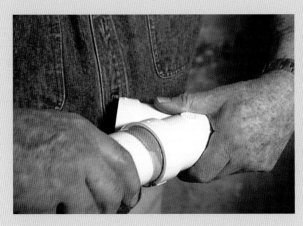

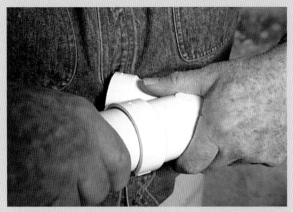

9 While the surfaces are still wet, I slip them together ...

10 ... give them a slight twist and hold them for a few seconds. If I don't hold them securely, the pipe and fitting can push away from each other.

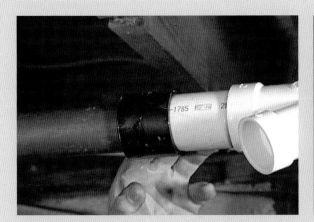

11 Should you need to join copper pipe to PVC, you can use what is referred to as a *mission clamp*. First I slide a metal clamp over the pipe. Then lubricate the pipe with dish washing detergent and slip on the rubber sleeve. The dish washing detergent acts as a lubricant and will not deteriorate the rubber.

12 Once I have the assembly in place, I pull the rubber sleeves over the joints, slip on the clamps and tighten them up.

Clearing a Dirty Aerator

**SLOW OR SPITTING SINKS MAY
JUST BE A FIVE-MINUTE FIX!**

The aerator in your sink is designed to spread the water stream into droplets. This saves water and reduces splashing. If the screen in the aerator clogs, the stream of water is affected.

1 The other day I came into the kitchen and turned on this faucet. Instead of a nice, smooth, bubbly stream of water, I got a lot of spitting and sputtering. I've seen this before. It almost always means debris is clogging the faucet aerator.

2 The fix is simple. First, I unscrewed the aerator ...

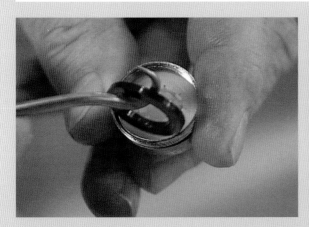

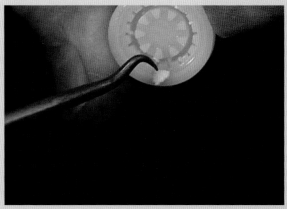

3 ... then take out the internal pieces paying attention to the order so I can reassemble the unit. ...

4 Sure enough, I find small white bits of material which I carefully picked out. If you live in an area with hard water, and don't use a water softener, this type of debris can be fairly common.

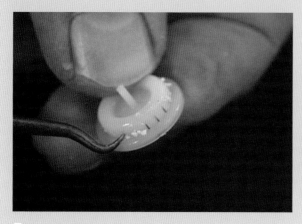

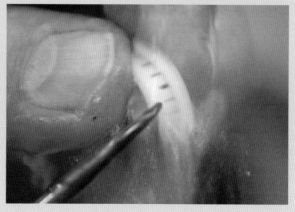

5 I use a small pick to remove the debris (a toothpick will work, also) ...

6 ... then wash the aerator thoroughly under running water.

7 I replace the aerator in the faucet fitting ...

8 ... and carefully screw it back in place.

9 No more sputter! Be aware, though, that if this happens once, it's likely to happen again and you may want to consider adding a water softener.

10 One more thing, kitchen faucets aren't the only place an aerator can clog. Your shower head can also accumulate debris.

11 As with the faucet, unscrew the shower head, and remove the debris, thoroughly cleaning the aerator.

12 Also, sediment can collect in a water heater from dirt, sand or minerals that are suspended in the water supply.

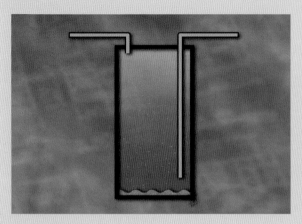

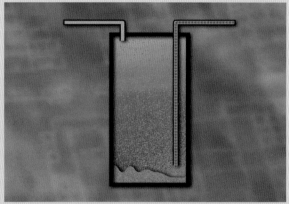

13 Over time, these deposits can build up quite an accumulation on the bottom of the tank, cutting down on burner efficiency.

14 Incoming water can stir up the sediment and send it to faucets, aerators, shower heads, dishwashers, clothes washing machines and any other water-using appliance in the house. If this is your situation, it's time to flush the water heater.

15 Start by turning your gas valve to the "pilot" position. If your heater is electric, turn off the circuit breakers. We do this because if the water level drops below the heating elements and the thermostat turns the elements on, the heating elements can be damaged.

16 Connect a hose to the spigot at the bottom of the water heater.

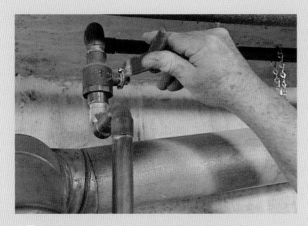

17 Shut off the incoming cold water ...

18 ... open a hot water faucet somewhere in the house ...

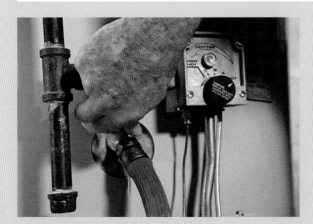

19 ... and then twist open the spigot on the water heater.

20 Out comes the water from the tank, along with any sediment. A ten-minute fix.

Unclogging a Drain

**A QUICK FIX FOR YOUR CLOGGED DRAIN
IS AS CLOSE AS YOUR P-TRAP**

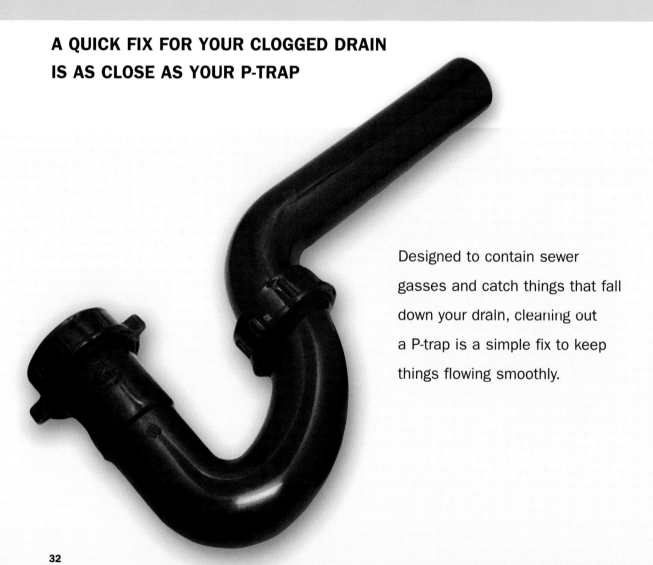

Designed to contain sewer gasses and catch things that fall down your drain, cleaning out a P-trap is a simple fix to keep things flowing smoothly.

1 I noticed this morning the drain was a little slow, but now it's stopped working altogether. So it's a problem I can't ignore any longer.

2 I have a few options available to me. I could try a plunger ...

3 ... or maybe get a small plumbing snake down in there ... or pour in some chemicals.

4 Before you resort to these measures, you may be able to find the solution under your nose ... or rather, under your sink. This is your P-trap. I'm not really sure why it's called a P-trap, since it's really shaped more like a "U".

5 This curvaceous piece of pipe serves two functions. It remains full of water, keeping sewer gasses from backing up into your sink. It's also a great catch-all for anything that goes down the drain. To remove a clog, first make sure you've got something to catch the water.

6 Unscrew the fitting attached to the sink drain ...

7 ... and then disconnect the side of the P-trap that leads to the waste pipe.

8 Like I said, make sure you put something underneath to catch the water!

9 P-traps can collect string, corn silk, pasta ...

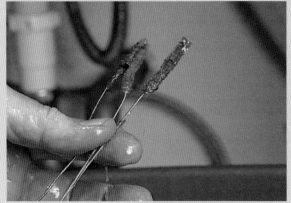

10 ... and those missing bottle brushes.

11 With the trap cleaned out, it's a quick chore to reattach the pipe ...

12 ... and get things flowing as they ought to.

Protect Pipes From Freezing

INSULATING PIPES IS ENERGY EFFICIENT AND EASY

Why insulate a water pipe? Well, I can think of three good reasons. It keeps cold water pipes from sweating, hot water pipes from losing heat and pipes running through unheated spaces from freezing.

1 This pre-slot polyethylene insulation is inexpensive and easy to install. Simply lay it over the pipe ...

2 ... peel back the protective covering ...

3 ... and press the two edges together. They are self sealing.

4 This flexible elastomeric insulation is similar but has a higher insulation value and is made with an antimicrobial for added defense against mold, often an issue with air conditioning and cold water pipes.

5 It's effective down to minus two hundred ninety-seven degrees Fahrenheit. Let's hope none of us will be testing that rating any time soon!

6 It installs the same as the polyethylene insulation. Wrap the pipe, expose the self-adhesive edges ...

7 ... and stick the two edges together.

8 Fiberglass insulation jackets are wrapped in a vapor barrier.

9   They're fairly rigid and can't be easily bent ...

10   ... but they can be painted with latex paint, an advantage if exposed pipes are running through a living area such as a finished basement.

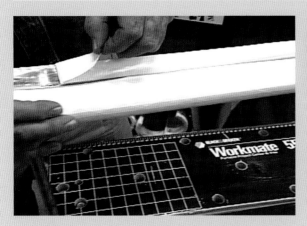

11   The installation is the same as the others. Peel ...

12   ... and stick.

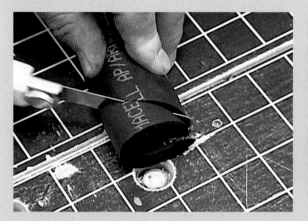

13 Cut miters on the ends of any of these tubular insulations ...

14 ... and fit the angles together to follow pipe bends.

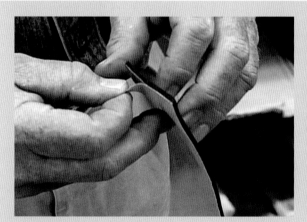

15 However, if you're facing several tightly-spaced bends, or you need to insulate a valve, this reinforced foam insulating tape might be the answer.

16 It's overlapped as it's applied ...

17 ... and will conform to just about any shape.

18 So I guess the question is not whether you should insulate your pipes, but what kind of insulation to use.

Perfect Caulk Application

**WITH MOST PLUMBING PROJECTS,
THE LAST STEP IS ADDING THE CAULK**

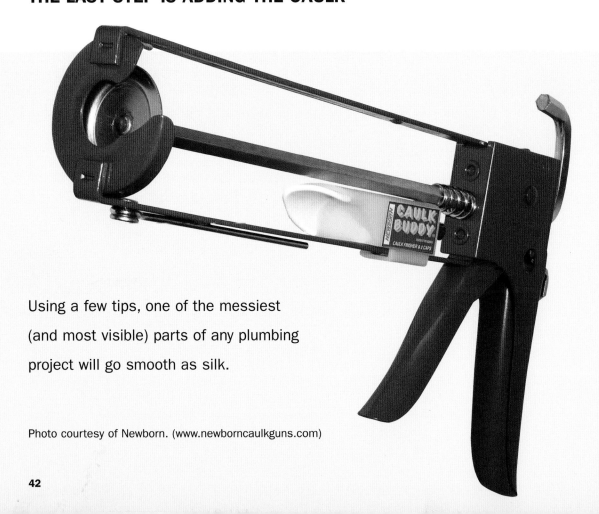

Using a few tips, one of the messiest (and most visible) parts of any plumbing project will go smooth as silk.

Photo courtesy of Newborn. (www.newborncaulkguns.com)

1 Caulks and sealants can be a sticky proposition but here are a few tips for you that will take the mess out of this job and give you results that are as smooth as a pro's.

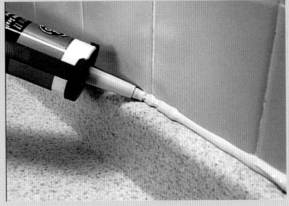

2 Messy caulk joints can be caused by putting down too much material in the first place.

3 When trying to smooth a joint, excess sealant oozes onto the surrounding surface. Cleaning it off takes time and often leaves ridges and ragged edges.

4 On the other hand, a caulk joint like this is easy to make if you keep a few tips in mind.

5 Caulks and sealants, especially silicone, work better at room temperature. If yours is stored in the garage or basement, bring it inside the night before and let it warm up. It will bond better and smooth more easily. Cut the cork tube nozzle at an angle close to the tip.

6 A smaller opening helps avoid over-filling the joint.

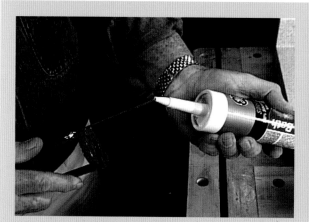

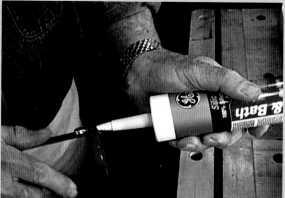

7 Many caulking guns have a built-in tool to pierce the seal at the base of the nozzle.

8 Simply extend the tool, and slide it all the way into the nozzle. You should feel the seal give way when it's pierced.

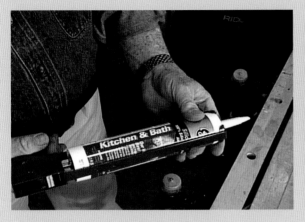

9 Choose a high-quality no-drip gun with a smooth trigger action.

10 Before applying sealant around a tub or sink, clean the surface with denatured alcohol.

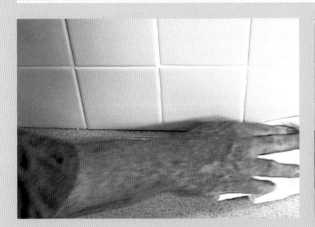

11 A quick swipe with the rag is all it takes.

12 Hold the caulking gun at a forty-five degree angle and pull it along the joint.

13 Lift it away quickly at the end of a pass.

14 Now the real secret to get a professional-looking smooth joint is something called tooling. That's where you take your finger and draw it over the caulk you just put down.

15 In the past, that's been a very messy job but there's a product on the market called Caulk-Mate that makes this go a lot smoother.

16 Caulk-Mate is sprayed onto the surface after applying the caulk.

17 It lubricates the surface, allowing me to apply enough pressure to push the caulk fully into the joint for a good seal.

18 At the same time, the solution prevents any excess sealant from sticking to the surface or my skin.

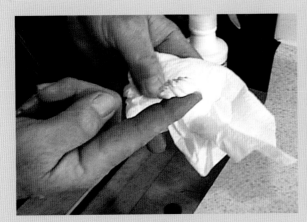

19 One wipe and my finger is as clean as a whistle. It's best if you can let silicone caulk sit overnight before using it.

20 If you've got the right technique and the right solution, you can get professional looking caulking results. Now you can tackle those caulking jobs that you may have been putting off.

SECTION TWO

Kitchens

Replacing a Faucet

**REPLACING A FAUCET IS NOT DIFFICULT AND
CAN ADD A NEW LOOK TO YOUR SINK.**

Sometimes, to spruce up the look or
change the style of your sink, all you
need to do is replace the faucet.

1 The first step in replacing a faucet is to turn off the water at the sink. Normally there would be shutoff valves right here to do just that.

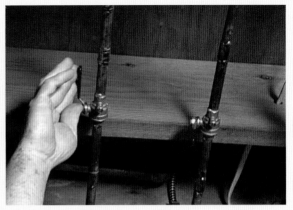

2 Since there are none, I end up in the basement having to turn off the water for the entire first floor.

3 By opening the faucet, I bleed off any remaining water pressure.

4 Next, I remove the sink drain, starting with the dishwasher hose. I unscrew the clamp at the drain connection first.

5 Then I simply slide the dishwasher hose off the pipe.

6 Next I disconnect the straight section of drain (called the tailpiece) connection at the sink drain.

7 Then I disconnect the drain and P-trap assembly.

8 I don't have to disconnect the drain, but doing so will give me a lot more room to work and easier access.

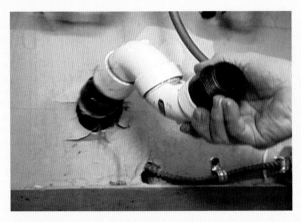

9 Finally I disconnect the last connections from the waste pipe going into the wall.

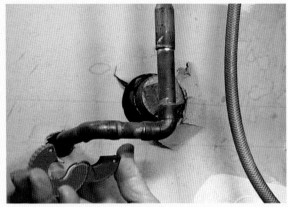

10 Next I cut the copper water lines where they come out of the wall.

11 This will make it possible to detach the lines from the faucet.

12 It's also where I'll install the shutoff valves so that from now on, the sink water supply can be turned off without affecting the rest of the house.

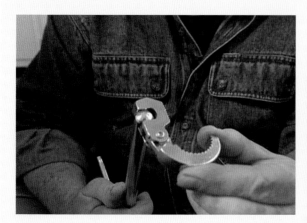

13 My next step is to unscrew those water lines that I just cut from the faucet. And that's where I find this tool to be indispensable.

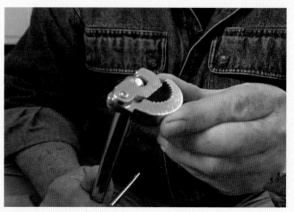

14 It's called a *basin wrench* and it's designed just for this purpose — to reach up behind the sink, grab that nut in these jaws and allow me to loosen it.

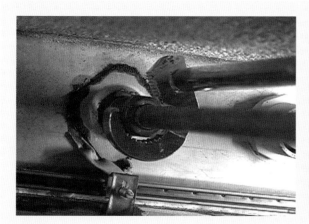

15 I'll show you what I mean. Now you can see how impossible it would be to get a conventional wrench in here. I use the tool in a sort of ratcheting motion, backing off the nut a fraction of a turn at a time ...

16 ... until I can remove it with my fingers.

17 I use this same tool to loosen the retaining nuts holding the faucet base to the sink.

18 Finally, with everything free ...

19 ... I can lift out the old faucet.

20 Underneath is quite a bit of dried plumber's putty which is cleaned up easily with a plastic putty knife.

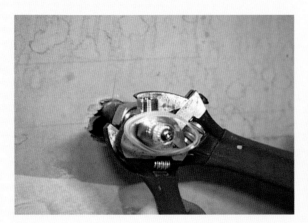

21 Well, I've gotten all of the old out and now I'm going to start putting the new in, beginning with these shutoff valves down below. I just slip the valves on the copper pipe and tighten the compression fittings, using two wrenches to avoid twisting the pipe.

22 The first step in installing the new fixture is to place a rubber "O" ring on the faucet base.

23 Then insert the lower end of the faucet into the sink hole. Underneath, I slip on a mounting plate and washer ...

24 ... followed by a retaining nut.

25 This plastic socket wrench comes with the fixture. To get the leverage I need, I insert a screwdriver to use as a handle.

26 Next I insert the spray nozzle hose into the end of the faucet ...

27 ... and push it all the way through and out the bottom.

28 This faucet has individual valves for hot and cold water. Plumber's putty will make a watertight seal at the valve base, preventing water from dripping into the cabinet below.

29 I'm ready to put in the valves. If this sink weren't already installed in the countertop, I could do this myself. But because it is already in place, I'm going to need some help. Peter shoves the valve up from below and I slip on a retaining ring.

30 As I apply pressure from above, Peter tightens the nuts from below.

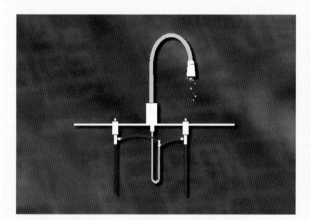

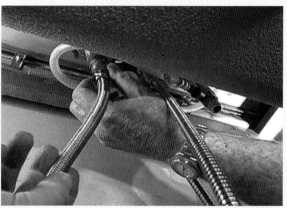

31 This is a two-valve faucet. When the valves are open, cold water flows through one and hot water through the other. Tubes connect the valves to the faucet hose where the hot and cold water are blended together and stream out through the nozzle.

32 On this faucet, the hoses connecting the faucet to the valves have clips that slip on and snap in place.

33 Next I connect the water supply lines, first to the faucet, using that basin wrench again ...

34 ... and then to the new shutoff valves.

35 Then I place the valve handles and trim on top of the valve body and screw them in place.

36 I drop the pump housing for the liquid soap dispenser in place ...

37 ... and secure it from the bottom with a retaining nut.

38 The pump sits on top so it can be lifted out for refilling.

39 With all the water supply lines connected, I can begin replacing the drain. Reinstalling this P-trap is about the last thing I'm going to have to do before I have to test for leaks.

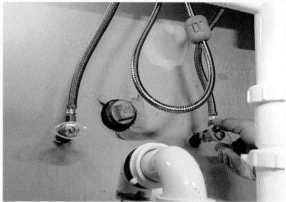

40 Well, everything's done. Now I can turn on the water and see if I've got any leaks.

41 I don't see or hear any water leaking. But here's my litmus test for leaks. I put some paper towels on the bottom of the cabinet and wait a few minutes. Then I come back and take a look. If there are any drops, they'll show up right here. So far, so good.

Installing a Stainless-Steel Sink

STILL A KITCHEN CROWD PLEASER, STAINLESS-STEEL SINKS ARE AN AFTERNOON PROJECT

If your kitchen is due for a facelift, a new counter and stainless steel sink may just be the ticket! Join me as I help Ed and Linda Raetz with their kitchen make-over.

1 Let's start by disconnecting the plumbing. First thing I want to do is turn off the water supply here. Shut off both the hot and cold water.

2 Next, turn on the faucet. If water is still coming out, I know that the shut-off valve isn't working properly. But, we're in good shape.

3 I'm going to put this pan in here to catch any water that might come out of this line as I disconnect it.

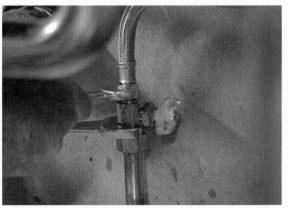

4 We'll disconnect the water lines here, using two wrenches. One to hold, the other to loosen the fitting.

5 With the fitting loose, I can finish removing the line by hand. Watch for water!

6 Next we're going to take the P-trap off by disconnecting both of the compression nuts. Again, watch for water. The pan will come in handy.

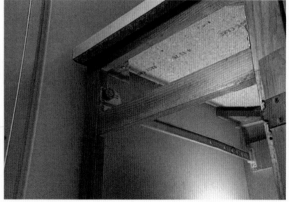

7 Usually countertops are held in place by screws and they're often found in the corners. Let's pull this drawer out and take a look.

8 Up here we have a block, with a screw in it going up into the countertop.

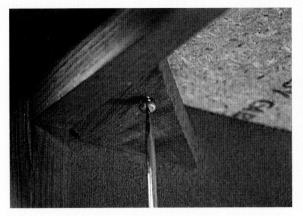

9 There are about a dozen screws to remove.

10 Everything should be loose, but let's give this a little bit of a test. Nope, not all loose.

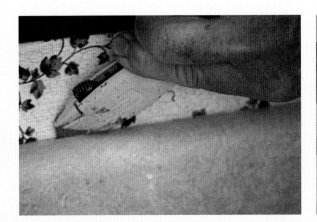

11 Sometimes backsplashes are caulked to the wall. We could tear it off, but we don't want to damage the wall. So we'll run a utility knife along the joint to cut at least the top of the caulk.

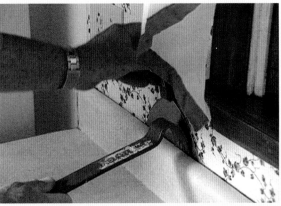

12 Next we gently pry the countertop loose. I'm using a putty knife behind the pry bar to protect the wall. In no time at all the countertop is loose.

13 We could have removed the sink from the countertop, but since we're replacing the sink, it's easier to carry the whole thing out in one piece.

14 The new laminate countertop came with the sink hole partially cut out already. But I want to make sure this is, in fact, the right size for our sink.

15 I cut the template out of the sink's packing box and place it over the countertop cutout. A good fit!

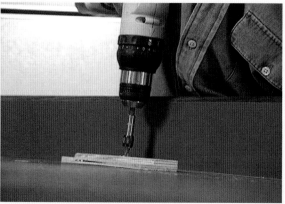

16 In order to keep the cutout from dropping when we saw through, we fashion a temporary clamp from two scraps of wood. Screwed in place in opposite corners on the bottom, and, on top of the counter, screwed into the cutout waste piece.

17 Linda uses a jigsaw to complete the cuts on the countertop.

18 As we unscrew our temporary clamps, the waste piece comes free and we have our completed sink opening.

19 After setting the new countertop in place and securing it with screws, we turn to the sink. It's a nice stainless-steel sink and we're going to do a few things to it before we lower it into the countertop.

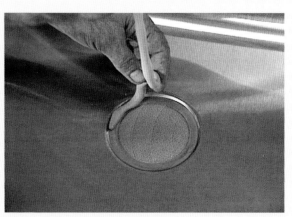

20 First, we apply plumber's putty to the edges of the drain cutouts.

21 We push the new sink baskets into the putty to create a watertight seal. The baskets are then held in place by screwing the mounting flange in place on the underside of the baskets.

22 Then, before installing the sink, we attach as much of the new plumbing as possible. Apply some plumber's putty on the underside of the faucets and screw the retaining nuts into place.

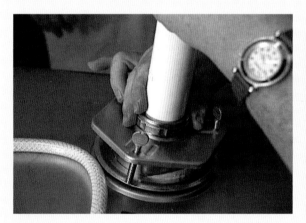

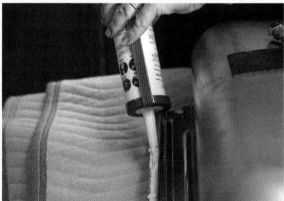

23 Even the drain pipe is attached to reduce the amount of work done under the counter.

24 Finally, we apply a silicone sealant around the sink lip to ensure a watertight bond with the countertop.

25 We lower the sink into place, as close to the finished position as possible, and allow the putty to squeeze out slightly.

26 Sometimes lying down on the job is inevitable. But someone has to tighten the clips that hold the sink to the countertop!

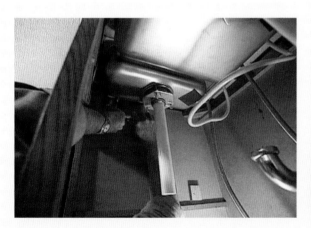

27 Two to three clips are used on each edge of the sink. The back can be a little awkward to reach, but don't skimp on the clips, because you want to be sure and get a good water-tight seal between the sink lip and the countertop.

28 With the drain and water connections completed, Ed and Linda are ready to put their new sink to work.

Installing a Cast-Iron Porcelain Sink

CAST-IRON SINKS ARE ANOTHER STYLE OF SINK THAT CAN GIVE A NEW LOOK TO YOUR KITCHEN

Cast-iron sinks will last for decades and are easy to install because they can be set in place and the rim sealed to the countertop. No clips to mess with like a stainless-steel sink.

1 The first step in removing the old sink is turning off the water at the shutoff valves located under the sink.

2 This pot will collect any water remaining in the lines when they're disconnected.

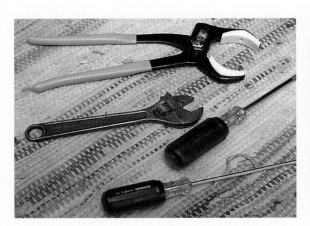

3 An adjustable wrench (center) is the best tool for this job, but we'll also be using adjustable multigroove pliers (top) and a couple of screwdrivers.

4 After loosening the nut holding the water-supply line to the shutoff valve with the pliers, unscrew the nut by hand.

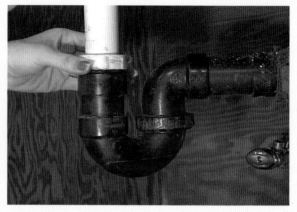

5 And that's why we put the pan under the sink!

6 Now we can disconnect the drain line. Some of these plastic nuts can be loosened by hand ...

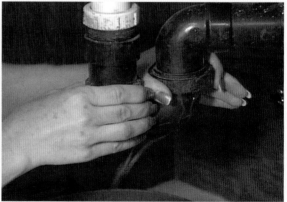

7 ... but others need a bit of coaxing and that will come from the adjustable multigroove pliers which open wide enough to grip the large nut.

8 This U-shaped piece of pipe known as the P-trap is always full of waste water. Pretty unappealing but it serves a purpose.

9 The water provides a seal that keeps the sewer gases from coming up through the sink. These gases can smell really bad.

10 Next, I unscrew these metal clips that attach the sink to the countertop.

11 All right, everyone grabs one side of the sink and we lift it right out.

12 We're ready to work on the new cast-iron sink. Porcelain on the top is very nice. To mount the faucet we start with this gasket that goes around the opening for the faucet to keep water from running into the hole and into the cabinet below. Next, we position the faucet's base plate.

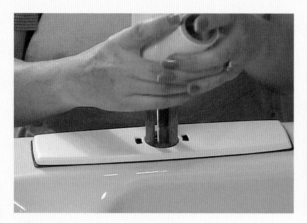

13 And, here's the single lever faucet. Part of it is missing right now. We'll put that in later. We drop the base piece down through the hole.

14 Jeff secures the faucet from the underside of the sink, first using spacers, then nuts.

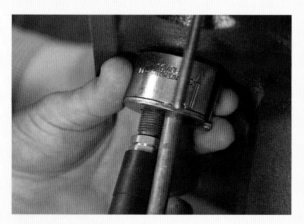

15 This black plastic socket wrench, made just for this purpose, comes packaged with the new faucet.

16 Two more studs hold the base plate tightly against the sink.

17 Next we slip the air gap device into the remaining hole.

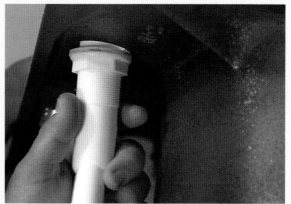

18 Its job is to prevent dirty sink water from siphoning into the dishwasher.

19 Now we thread the end of the faucet wand hose right down through the faucet base and down through the bottom.

20 Then screw the end in place.

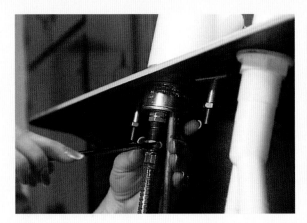

21 Ann screws the water hose for the wand onto a fitting on the underside of the faucet.

22 Then she and Jeff attach a lead weight to the hose. The weight will help the hose retract back into the faucet when it's not in use.

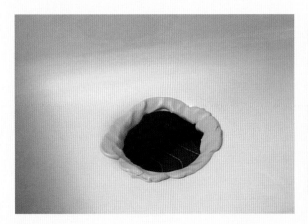

23 This is plumber's putty. I've formed it into a coil and laid it around the sink drain opening. You don't have to be too fussy with this because the excess is going to squeeze out.

24 The putty is used as a seal for the strainer basket. Okay, now we grab the basket and just shove it in there, pressing it down with our fingers.

25 We flip the sink over and install the hardware that will secure the basket strainer in place. First is the rubber gasket, then a cardboard gasket.

26 And finally a retaining ring. This wrench is designed just for tightening these nuts.

27 With everything attached, our sink is a bit heavy, but Jeff and I carefully place it through the opening in the countertop. We rest the sink on wood blocks.

28 The blocks serve two purposes — to keep us from pinching our fingers ...

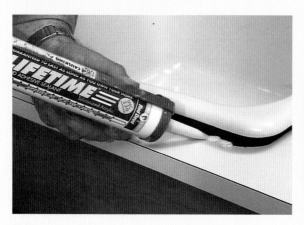

29 ... and allow us to easily caulk the countertop.

30 Jeff supports the sink from the bottom while I put down the final strip of caulking. Then, we carefully lower the sink into place.

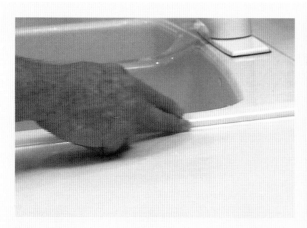

31 Smoothing the caulk is best done with a finger dipped in soapy water.

32 Finally, with the sink in position, we begin reinstalling the plumbing, starting with the water supply lines ...

33 ... then the drain connections.

34 Finally we turn on the water and check for leaks.

35 Everything is dry, tight and working fine!

Installing a Prep Sink

**IF YOU HAVE THE SPACE, THIS IS A
NICE ADDITION TO YOUR KITCHEN.**

If you've got a large kitchen and do a lot of cooking at home, you may find the need for a second sink. That's our situation, and this prep sink mounted in our island nicely fits the bill.

1 My prep sink is going in an existing granite countertop, so I got some professional help to cut the opening, but the process is the same in any top material. Use the template provided with the sink to mark and then cut the opening.

2 With the sink hole cut, the ultimate test is to drop the sink in and see if it's the right size! It fits and the hole is just slightly oversized which is exactly the what we want.

3 With the sink in position, I lower a plumb bob through the center of the drain hole ...

4 ... and mark the location directly beneath on the cabinet's bottom.

5 Then, using an extra-long drill bit, I bore through the bottom of the cabinet ...

6 ... and into the basement below.

7 Down in the basement I can see where the drill came through. That's the center of the sink opening. I'm in pretty good shape because I have a cold water line right here, a hot water line here ...

8 ... and a drain right over here. So everything is in fairly close proximity.

9 Because I've put in shutoff valves for the kitchen and laundry room, I don't have to turn off the water to the entire house.

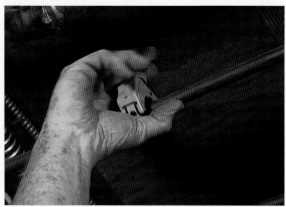

10 The first step in tapping into the existing water supply is to cut the copper water lines with a small pipe cutter that works very well in tight quarters like these.

11 Watch the water! Even though the water is shut off, there's usually a little left in the lines.

12 Then I make a second cut and remove a small section of pipe.

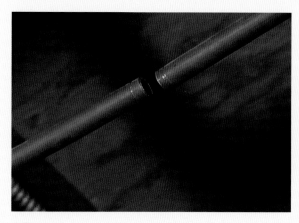

13 This will give me the space I need to install the "T" fittings I'll be putting in shortly.

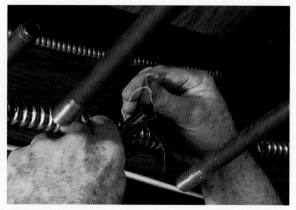

14 I'm sanding the pipe to remove any surface dirt and oxidation. This is the first step in getting a watertight solder joint.

15 With the pipe clean, I next apply soldering flux.

16 This paste helps the solder flow evenly and promotes a good bond with the metal.

17 The inside of the fittings also need cleaning. I do this with a metal brush made just for this purpose.

18 Once I finish the cleaning, I coat the fitting with the flux.

19 Now I can slip the pieces together.

20 I clean and add flux to each of the fittings as I assemble them. We'll make them permanent when everything is in place.

21 Now I'm turning my attention to the drain.

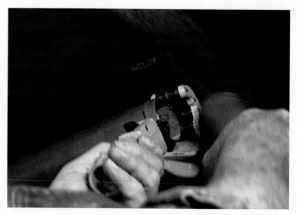

22 Slicing through this guy calls for a bigger pipe cutter.

23 For this project, I'm removing about a foot of pipe. The new drain line will be PVC plastic pipe that's glued or welded together.

24 I first apply a purple primer to both the fitting and the pipe followed by an application of PVC cement.

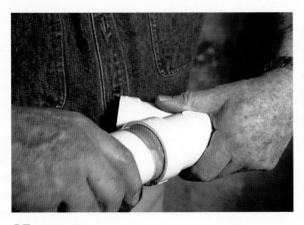

25 While the surfaces are still wet, I slip them together, give them a slight twist and hold them for a few seconds.

26 This "Y" assembly will allow the sink drain to join the existing drain line.

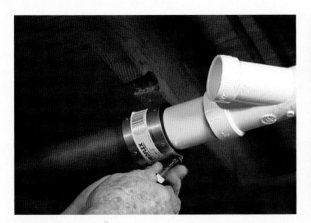

27 To join the existing copper drain to the PVC, I use a *mission clamp* (a rubber sleeve that crosses both sections) and a metal band clamp to hold it all together.

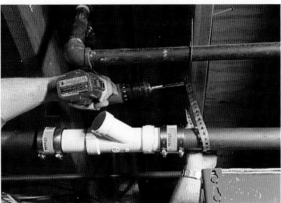

28 This perforated copper hanging strap will support the drain pipe, taking the strain off the coupling.

29 Now I'm back upstairs drilling the holes for the water supply lines. This long shaft spade bit is the perfect tool for this.

30 Next I move on to the drain. Here, I'm using a two-inch hole saw with a shaft extension. I'm doing the best I can to make sure the drill bit stays as vertical as possible.

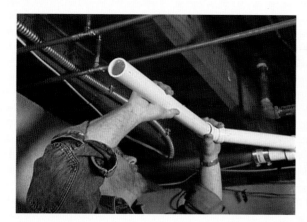

31 Now I need to put in the run of pipe that will connect the drain and the water supply lines to the sink. I want to do a dry fit first to make sure that all the pipes are cut to the proper lengths.

32 I'll go back and cement or solder it in place.

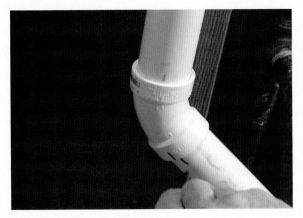

33 Before I disassemble the pieces, I make reference marks so I can put them back together in the same position.

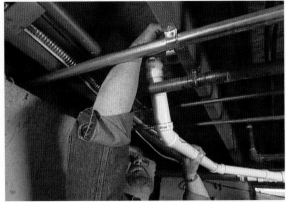

34 Then I glue the assembly together, attaching one end to the riser that goes into the kitchen cabinet...

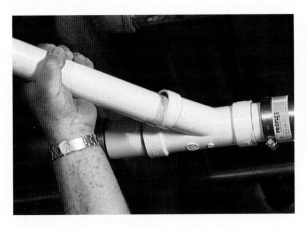

35 ... and the other to the "Y" in the drain.

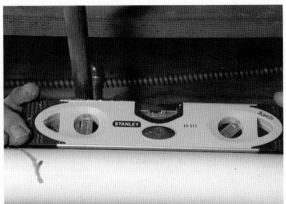

36 Finally, I check to make sure there's a gradual downward slope to the drain.

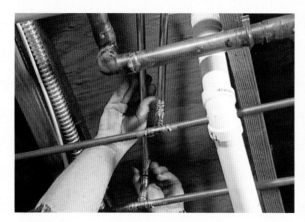

37 Now I can fit the copper pipes together. For this project, I'm using pre-soldered fittings. The solder is already inside.

38 All I have to do is add heat. When things get hot enough, the solder liquefies and begins to flow out of the joint. You can see it here and here.

39 Now I have to add some fittings on the sink end. First I'm installing what's called a sanitary "T". The sink drain will attach to this later.

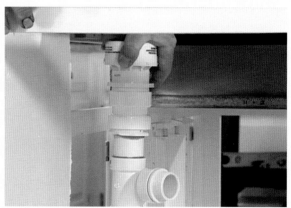

40 Above the "T" goes a vent.

41 And at the bottom, a trim escutcheon.

42 Next, I cut off the water lines ...

43 ... and install escutcheons on these.

44 Then I slip on the shutoff valves and tighten the compression fittings using a wrench.

45 I always loved modeling clay as a kid. This is about as close as I can get to it in home improvement!

46 It's plumber's putty, a mixture of oil and minerals like limestone and clay. Plumber's putty has been around for ages and it seems to last forever. It's what I use to seal the sink basket to the sink.

47 On the underside of the sink, I Place a rubber seal, an anti-friction fiber washer and the lock nut.

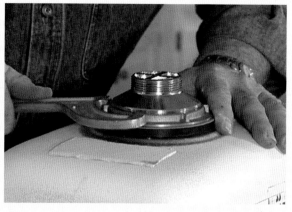

48 This basin nut-wrench has only one purpose in life. And this is it.

49 With the basket snugly in place, I lift off the excess plumbers putty.

50 To install my new faucet, I drop the water lines through the hole, flip the sink over and slip on a mounting plate.

51 I screw on a nut ...

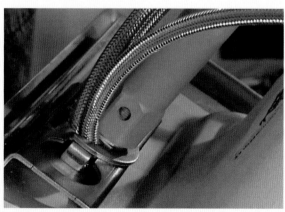

52 ... and then tighten it up using a plastic socket that came with the faucet set.

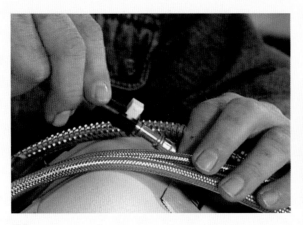

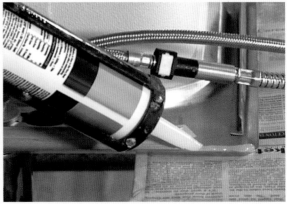

53 Next I pass the sprayer hose through the center of the faucet and connect it on the underside.

54 I'm ready to drop the sink in the opening. I just need to put some silicone sealant around the edge.

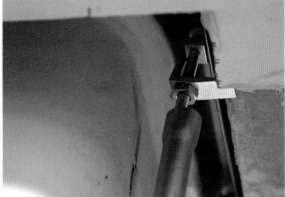

55 This type of sink drops in from the top (it's called self-rimming). The watertight seal around the edge comes from the silicone ...

56 ... and these clamps on the bottom side that pull the sink down into firm contact with the countertop when they're tightened.

57 To make the last few hookups on the drain, I attach this tailpiece to the bottom of the sink basket ...

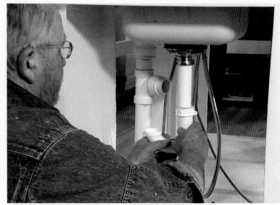

58 ... slip on the P-trap ...

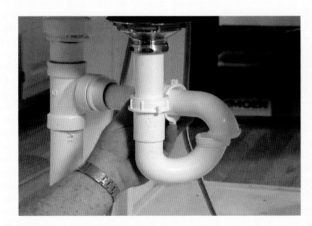

59 ... and connect everything to the drain system.

60 On the water supply side, all I have to do is screw on the lines from the faucet, snug them up with a wrench and turn on the water. Another successful plumbing project!

Replacing a Disposal

DISPOSE OF THE OLD ONE, INSTALL A NEW ONE

If your present disposal has seen better days, it's probably time to replace it. This is not a difficult job. Just a few days ago, a friend named Natalie called to complain that her disposal had died. She'd already bought a nearly identical unit, but needed a hand with the installation. No problem!

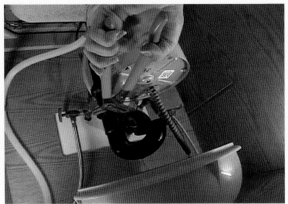

1 With most plumbing jobs, the first step is to turn off the water. But with a disposal, no water is actually being supplied to the device. It is important to remember that the disposal is hooked up to electricity. Kill the power at the breaker and disconnect the wires.

2 Next, we turn to the plumbing, and remove the P-trap from the connection at the wall ...

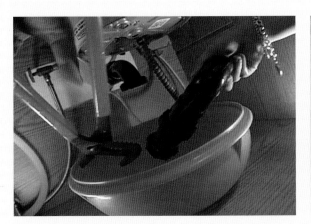

3 ... and the disposal. I've got a pan handy to catch the water that's guaranteed to be in the P-trap.

4 Next we disconnect the drain line from the dishwasher to the disposal.

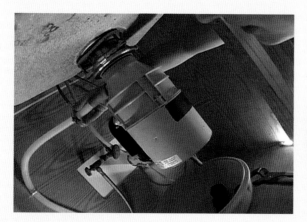

5 These lines are most commonly held in place with a hose clamp. Once the clamp is loosened, the line will slide off the fitting on the disposal.

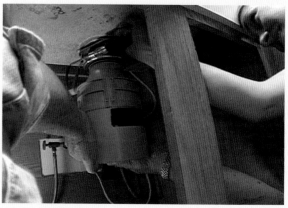

6 To remove the disposal from the drain basket, we need to release the mounting collar.

7 The collar has loops positioned in a few place around the perimeter. Simply slip a screwdriver through one of the loops, and a quarter, or half-turn of the collar will release the disposal.

8 Then just hang on to things and bring the disposal out from under the counter. After taking a closer look at Natalie's sink, I convince her we might as well replace it also. A quick trip to the home center store and we're ready to continue.

9 We've got the new sink sitting on a pad on the floor and Natalie starts attaching the drain fittings by moulding plumber's putty to the underside of the drain flange. Then the flange is slid through the hole in the sink.

10 Then we slip on a fiber gasket ...

11 ... a backup ring ...

12 ... and a mounting ring.

13 The snap ring holds everything in place.

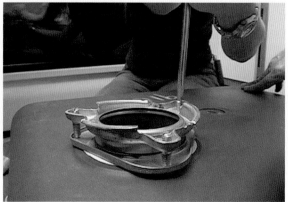

14 Finally the entire assembly is tightened securely to the sink by tightening three set screws. As the screws are turned the strainer basket is pulled tightly to the sink.

15 Now we just use our fingers to remove the excess plumber's putty that has squeezed out around the strainer basket flange.

16 With the new mounting collar installed, the new disposal is lifted up into place under the sink and slipped into the collar.

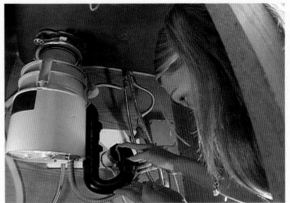

17 Natalie reconnects the dishwasher drain connection to the disposal, reattaches the wiring ...

18 ... and finally places the P-trap in place. The disposal is complete. It takes only a few more minutes to hook up the new faucet (yes, we bought one of those, too).

19 Well, our simple disposal replacement became a little larger project, but the time went quickly and the job looks great.

Replacing a Dishwasher

MORE THAN JUST AN ELECTRICAL PROJECT, IT'S ONE THAT YOU CAN TACKLE ON YOUR OWN AND SAVE MONEY

Sandi Fix just moved into her first home and one of the first upgrades she wanted to tackle was replacing the outdated dishwasher that was noisy and rattled. I told her I'd give her a hand.

1 Like many first-time homeowners, Sandi fix knows her new house needs a lot of work. One of the first things she wants to tackle is replacing the aging dishwasher. It's noisy and just doesn't work the way that it should anymore.

2 We start by turning off the power at the breaker box.

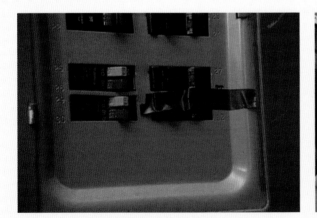

3 Then, tape down the switch so no one will come along and accidentally turn it on a again.

4 We remove the access plate at the bottom part of the appliance where all the plumbing and electrical connections are. This may be attached with a screw or bolt or simply snapped in place.

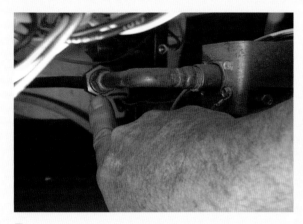

5 The water line attaches to the dishwasher here ...

6 ... the electrical is coming in here ...

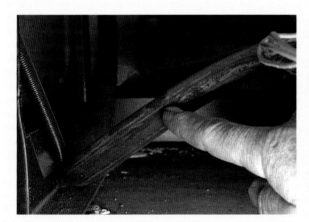

7 ... and this is the drain hose here.

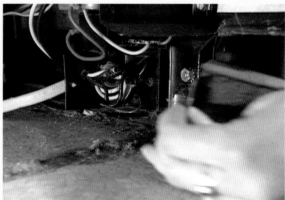

8 After shutting off the water supply, our next job is to remove the cover to access the electrical lines.

9 We test the wires to make sure that they're not live.

10 No noise from our tester, so we can go ahead and cut them.

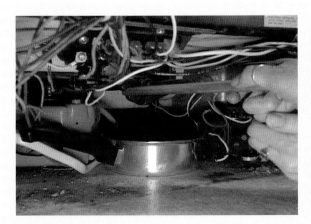

11 We slip a pan under the water connection as there may be a little bit of water leaking out. Then Sandi loosens up the connection on the water line using the perfect tool for tight spaces ...

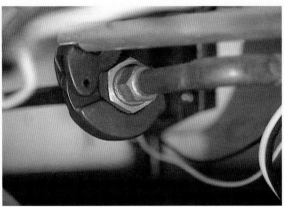

12 ... the basin wrench.

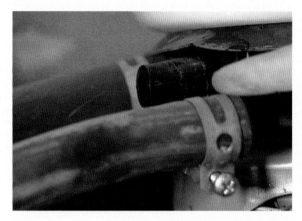

13 Then she moves on to disconnect the drain line. First she releases the clamp, then with a slight tug pulls the hose free.

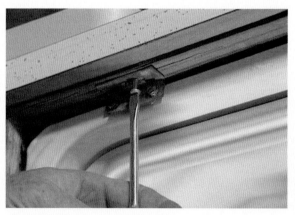

14 Now that all of our major connections are separated, we can detach the dishwasher from the cabinet.

15 We each take a side of the old dishwasher and wiggle it a little to get it pulled out from the cabinet space. As appliances go, dishwashers aren't all that heavy, but they can be awkward.

16 It's also smart to pull the old appliance out slowly to make sure you're not caught on anything that could be pulled loose.

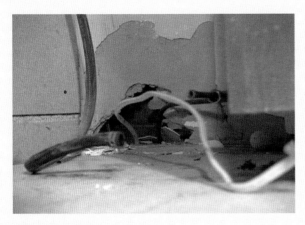

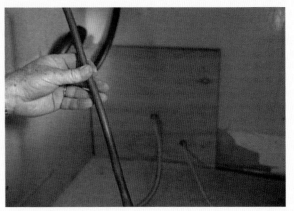

17 Once the dishwasher is removed, we can easily work in the space.

18 So, with the dishwasher out of the way, I replace the old copper tubing ...

19 ... with new flexible water lines.

20 We're ready to install Sandi's new dishwasher. She removes the access panel at the bottom of the new dishwasher so that we can get to all of the connection points.

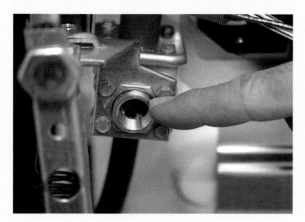

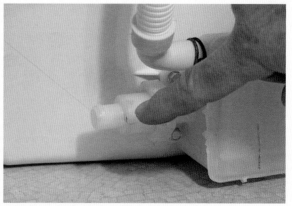

21 Installing the new dishwasher is going to be easy. We'll attach the water supply line right here, ...

22 ... the drain hose here ...

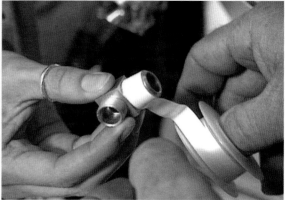

23 ... and make the electrical connections inside this box.

24 But before we do that, we have to install a couple fittings, beginning here on the water supply lines. We're going to first wrap the fitting with Teflon tape, which is used to help make the plumbing seal tight.

25 It acts as a lubricant helping the threads make better contact, thus preventing leaks. Without it you might get what plumbers call a false tight ...

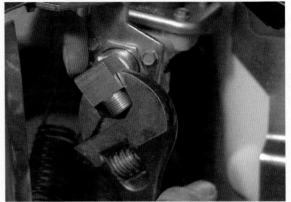

26 ... where it feels tight but really it isn't tight enough.

27 We'll be making our electrical connections inside this box. First, we're installing what's called a strain relief.

28 It will hold the electrical cable securely to the box and help prevent it from being accidentally pulled out. First hand-tighten the nut, then snug it up with a pair of pliers.

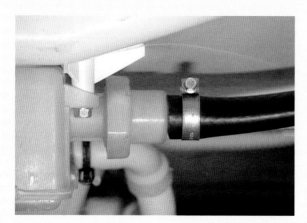

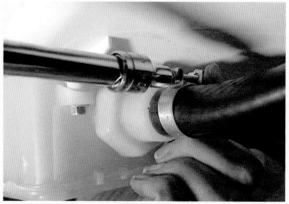

29 We're ready to install our new dishwasher. Let's start with the drain line. It's easier to make the drain connection while the dishwasher is out of the cabinet. First, we slip in the drain hose, then slide a hose clamp into position.

30 Then, tighten the clamp ...

31 ... and slide the dishwasher under the counter, making sure that we don't ruffle up the insulation that surrounds it.

32 We level the dishwasher ...

33 ... by screwing the front legs in or out.

34 There are two mounting tabs at the top of the dishwasher. We run screws through these to secure the unit to the underside of the countertop.

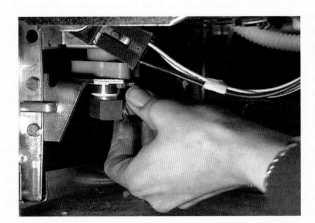

35 Underneath the dishwasher, Sandi reconnects the water supply line ...

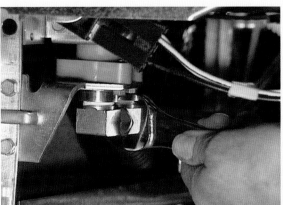

36 ... making sure the nut is wrenched tight.

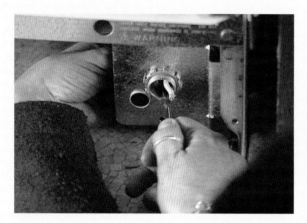

37 Then we move on to the final connection — the electric wires. First we pass the electrical cable through the strain relief.

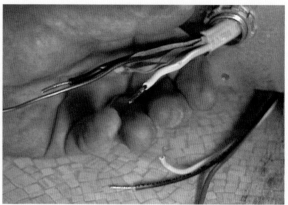

38 Then we strip the wires, leaving about one half inch exposed ...

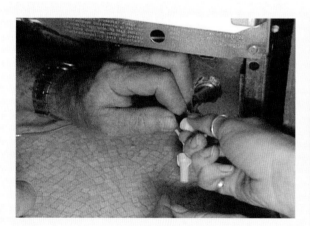

39 ... then connect them according to the manufacturer's instructions.

40 The last thing we do is replace the cover on the electrical box.

41 Now we can reinstall the access panel.

42 One last screw and then we can turn on the power and water.

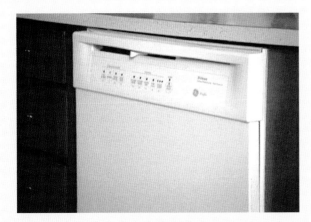

43 We set a couple of switches and give it a test. It's working great and it's quiet — no rattles. While this is a fairly involved home improvement, it's worth the time and effort.

Bathrooms

Installing a Bathroom Sink

**SIMPLY REPLACING YOUR BATHROOM SINK CAN
GIVE YOUR BATHROOM A NEW LOOK.**

Laura Allen wanted to replace her
bathroom sink and bring her bathroom
into the 21st century.

1 Laura Allen of Mobile, Alabama loves her historic city, but her 1970s bathroom vanity? That's a bit of history she's ready to replace.

2 The countertop looks outdated, and the sink is badly worn and scratched. So today, Laura and I are embarking on a vanity makeover.

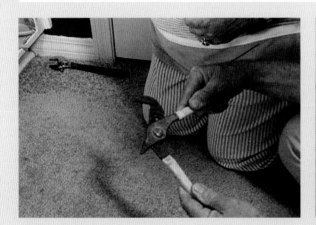

3 After shutting off the water at the valves located under the sink, I grab a pair of wide mouth, multi-groove pliers and head for the plumbing connections.

4 We start by disconnecting the P-trap from the sink and waste pipe. Keep a pan handy to catch the water!

5 Next we disconnect the water supply lines using an adjustable wrench.

6 The backsplash for the sink is caulked to the wall, so to remove the top without damaging the wall we run a utility knife along the backsplash to cut through the paint and caulk.

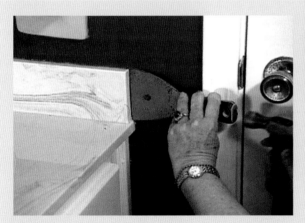

7 Then Laura separates the backsplash from the wall by gently hammering a putty knife between the two to break the adhesive bond.

8 A pry bar pops the top loose and we're ready to take it out of the bathroom.

9 Our new countertop is cultured marble. Well, it's not really marble, it's synthetic, but it looks good. It's been cut by the factory to the right length for our alcove. We also had the sink opening and faucet holes bored, which I recommend.

10 And this is our porcelain enamel sink. It's going to drop right in the hole like this. We'll seal it in place once the top is in the bathroom.

11 When I install a new countertop, I always like to put in the fixtures beforehand. Everything is easier to see and reach. Laura connects the water lines to the shutoff valves ...

12 ... and the mixing valve to the faucet.

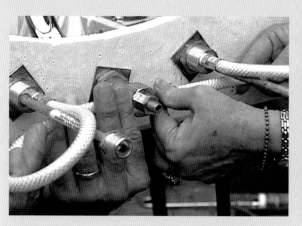

13 Hoses then connect the shutoff valves to the faucet mixer.

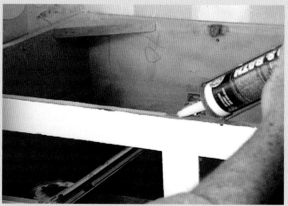

14 Next, we run a bead of silicone along the top edge of the base cabinet.

15 Then I lay a couple of wooden dowels across the cabinet top.

16 This allows us to slide the countertop across the dowels without disturbing the bead of silicone.

17 Once it's in place, we pull the dowels out and the countertop drops on top of the sealant.

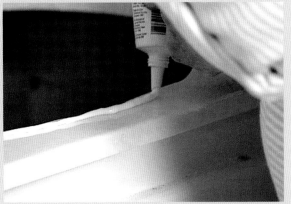

18 Next, Laura runs a bead of white silicone around the sink opening ...

19 ... and then the two of us carefully lower the sink into position.

20 All that's left is reattaching the drain and reconnecting the water supply lines to the shutoff valves coming out of the wall and the bathroom is back in business.

Repairing a Toilet

TOILETS ARE A STANDARD BATHROOM FIXTURE THAT YOU ONLY NEED BASIC SKILLS TO REPAIR

Water can be really difficult to live with, sometimes it runs when you don't want it to, and then it won't run right when you do want it to. Take my toilet for example. The last few days it's been running on its own. When it happened the first time in the middle of the night, I thought it might be one of those shadowy visitors that goes bump in the dark.

1 Let me just show you how a toilet works. When I push the flush lever, this arm, attached to a chain, comes up ...

2 ... and that chain, lifts up the flapper valve on the bottom of the tank. When that happens, all the water that's in the tank flows into the toilet bowl, and that's what does the flushing.

3 My problem here, I'm pretty sure, is that the seal between the flapper and the seat is faulty.

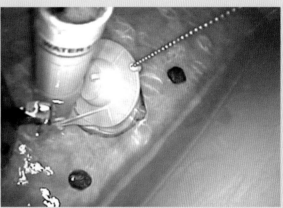

4 There could be some dirt in there ...

123

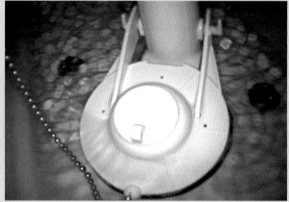

5 ... some corrosion that could have left a little ridge on the flapper.

6 I'm not even certain that that's the problem. But there is one way I can find out.

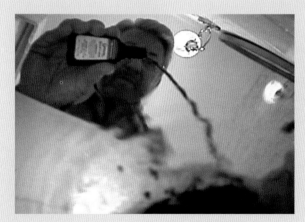

7 I'm going to put a few drops of food coloring in the tank.

8 If there is water leaking through that valve, then we'll begin to see a little bit of the green dye or food coloring showing up in the toilet bowl.

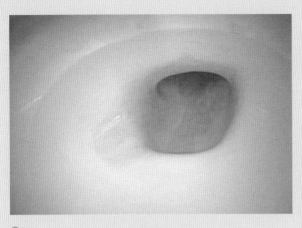

9 Let's take a look, yep, sure enough, you can see that dye just sort of trickling in there.

10 Well, that's water, that's coming into the bowl, so every once in a while, the tank level gets to a low point, and the valve turns on and refills the tank; and that goes on over and over and over.

11 The result is an annoying sound and a big waste of water. It is possible to replace just the flapper valve, but the problem for us will be in the seat. I've found that it's usually better just to replace the entire flushing mechanism. It doesn't take very long, is inexpensive and will guarantee me years of trouble-free service.

12 Step number one is turn off the water supply to the tank.

13 Then I flush the toilet. The water in the tank drains out, but doesn't refill. By holding the flapper open, most of the water will drain out.

14 However, there's always a bit of residual water left and the best way to get that out is with a sponge and a bucket.

15 Next I disconnect the water supply line from the bottom of the tank.

16 Then I get ready to disconnect the tank from the toilet base. It's held on with three bolts. You can see the heads on them down here. With a screwdriver from above ...

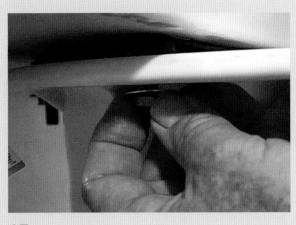

17 ... and a wrench, and then finger from below, I remove the three bolts,

18 With the bolts out, the tank just lifts off.

19 Next, using multi-groove pliers, I loosen the large nut holding the valve seat to the tank ...

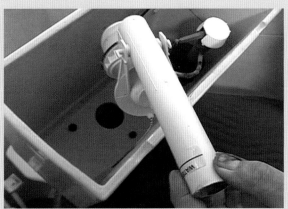

20 ... and remove the valve seat and overflow tube assembly.

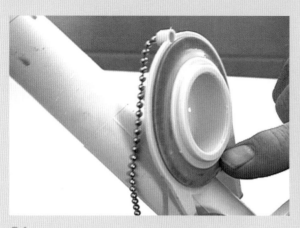

21 Maybe the seal here has gotten hard, maybe there are some calcium deposits. When I look at the flapper I can see that it's not a good seal, so bye, bye.

22 Then I remove the gasket from the bottom of the tank.

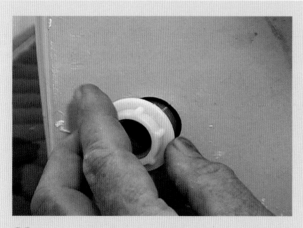

23 Next I remove the flush valve, starting with the nylon nut on the bottom of the tank.

24 Although this is a fairly new model, I've got some mineral deposits here too, so I'm just going to replace this as well.

25 In a matter of ten or fifteen minutes, I've been able to strip everything off the tank and now I'm ready to rebuild it.

26 This is the new flapper valve and seat.

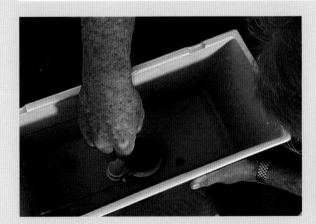

27 I'm going to insert this down into the tank ...

28 ... and screw the nut on the bottom.

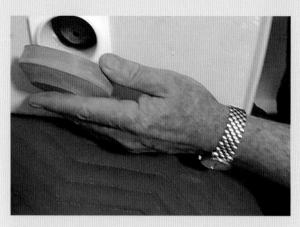

29 This new gasket, which is part of the repair kit, slips over the nut.

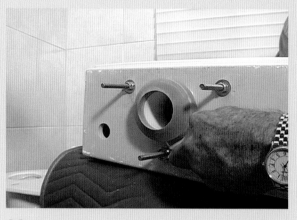

30 Next I install the bolts, nuts and washers that secure the tank to the bowl.

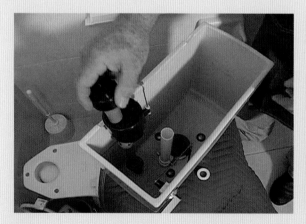

31 Now I'll drop in the new flush valve through the smaller hole in the bottom of the tank.

32 The flush valve is held in place with a nylon nut. I want this snug, but I'm careful not to over tighten it.

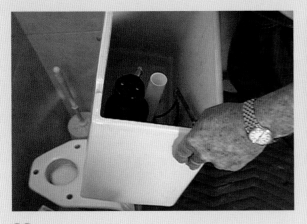

33 Now I'm ready to set the tank back in place, aligning the three bolts with the holes in the base.

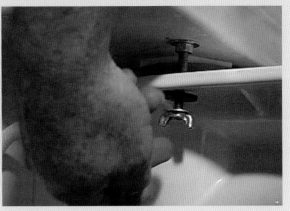

34 Rubber, then metal washers are slipped over the bolts and wing nuts are screwed on.

35 Finally I reattach the water line, turn on the valve and put the cover back on the tank. The tank is filling fine, and stops filling (I'll adjust the water height and the chain length in a minute, following the directions that come with the kit).

36 But first ... ah, a successful flush, and no running water!

Replacing a Toilet

SOMETIMES YOU NEED TO REPLACE THE ENTIRE TOILET

Newlyweds Kelly and Kate Miller spend their weekends planning all sorts of renovations. Yet there's one home improvement project they've been reluctant to face alone. So today, I'm here to lend a hand replacing their toilet.

1 Their toilet has a couple of problems. It's crooked and cracked off at an angle.

2 And it also has a hole in the base.

3 Our first step is to turn off the water supply to the tank. The shut off valve is located on the wall behind the toilet.

4 Then we remove the water from the tank by flushing ...

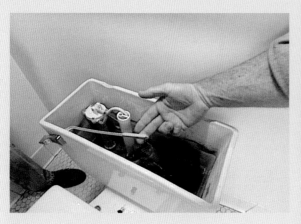

5 ... and holding the drain valve up.

6 We'll soak up the rest of the water with a sponge.

7 Since we're replacing the whole toilet, we also need to get the water out of the bottom of the bowl. Again, a sponge does the trick.

8 With all of the water emptied out, Kate loosens the nut that attaches the water line to the tank and pulls the line free.

9 The toilet is held down to the floor with two bolts that are hidden beneath these decorative covers. The existing bolts are badly rusted. In fact, these bolts have rusted completely through, leaving only the bead of caulk holding the toilet in place.

10 We use a utility knife to cut through the caulking at the bottom of the base..

11 And up comes the old toilet.

12 What we have left is the wax ring.

13 It's made of bee's wax. Kind of a simple, primitive idea but it works. It makes a very good seal between the bottom of the toilet and this flange in the floor. Not very attractive looking.

14 Kelly and Kate remove the wax ring using putty knives, then scrape the remaining wax from the flange.

15 Before we bring in the new toilet, Kate replaces the water supply line. I always recommend this when installing a new sink or toilet. Older lines often lose their seal after being disturbed.

16 This is the new wax ring. It's got a plastic rim on one side, and that side always faces away from the toilet.

17 Next we pack some plumber's putty into the slots on the flange.

18 The putty will help hold these two mounting bolts upright.

19 Kelly and I lower the new toilet into place so that the bolts extend through the holes in the base. When in position we apply pressure on the base, pushing straight down (no wiggling) to compress the wax ring and give us our seal.

20 Next, Kelly slips a nut cover base over each bolt, followed by a washer and nut.

21 These bolts are pre-scored, so the excess length can be snapped off with a pair of pliers. Had they not been scored, we would have cut them with a hacksaw.

22 With the bolts at to the right height, the nut cover snaps in place on the cover base.

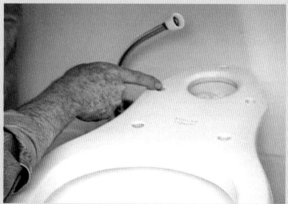

23 Next, we next move on to the water tank. Three bolts are extending through the bottom and the gasket is in place.

24 Next we lift the tank into place, aligning the bolts with the holes.

25 With the bolts extending through the base, we hold each one steady with a screwdriver from inside the tank ...

26 ... while we slip on a washer and nut from below ...

27 ... and then tighten the nut with a socket wrench. We can now reattach the water line to the tank, but we'll wait to turn the water back on.

28 One thing that might not be obvious is to check that your tank is level. When it's level, the water will empty the tank more efficiently (and it looks better!).

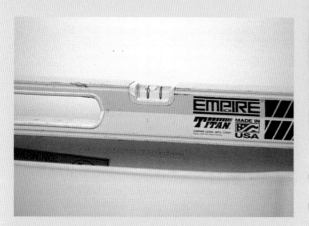

29 We use a small torpedo level on the back of the tank, and tighten the tank base nut on the high side, compressing the rubber gasket a little more.

30 The toilet seat is simple to install. But, there is a little trick. The seat is attached with a nylon bolt which straps through a hole in the base.

31 And even though it doesn't look like it, the lower piece is a nut.

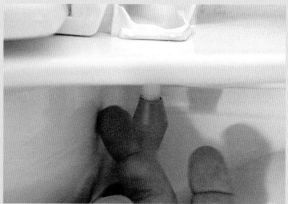

32 It's a cylindrical nut that will jam itself into this hole in the base and won't spin around as it's tightened. I usually start these by screwing a nut on the bottom like this.

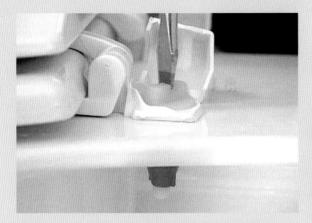

33 But you can't finish tightening it from the bottom. There's a slot here in the top, so we drop a screwdriver in here. The nut will not spin because of the way it's shaped — it's biting into the inside of that hole now.

34 With the seat tightened, the bolt is covered with a snap-on cap.

35 Finally the crowning moment. We put the tank lid in place and turn on the water. Everything flushes fine, no leaks — and a much better look.

Tankless Water Heaters

A TANKLESS WATER HEATER WILL GIVE YOU HOT WATER ON DEMAND, THUS SAVING YOU WATER-HEATING FUEL COSTS

Before you replace your worn out water heater, look at a tankless water heating system and see if it could work for you.

1   A water heater can be expected to last about eight to twelve years. The first sign yours may be nearing the end of its life span is when it takes longer than normal for hot water to reach your faucet.

2   The years seemed about right, so I headed to the home improvement store to check my options. Bernard listens to my story and then directs me to a tankless water heater, telling me the smaller unit can produce just as much water as a traditional tank at less cost.

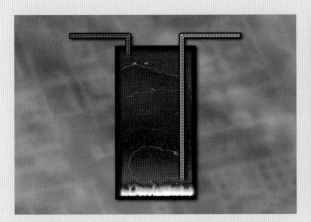

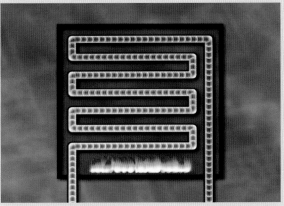

3   Bernard explains that a conventional water heater works by keeping a tank full of water continually hot and ready for use.

4   Tankless versions, on the other hand, only heat water on demand. When hot water is turned on anywhere in the house, the unit starts and water is brought up to temperature instantaneously as it continuously flows through the internal heat exchanger.

5 I'm sold. So I load my tankless water heater onto a cart and into my truck. Now, being the do-it-yourself type, I entertained thoughts of installing it myself and perhaps I could have, but in the end, I opt for professional help.

6 Once I watched the professional crew remove this ...

7 ... and spend the day install this (rerunning plumbing and gas lines), I knew I'd made the right decision. One of the obvious benefits of this system is replacing a massive tank in my basement with a compact unit that's up out of the way on the wall.

8 But the real payoff is that I will now have enough hot water to wash the dishes ...

9 ... give the kids a bath ...

10 ... and take a shower, all at the same time.

11 In addition to the main thermostat, I also have a bedroom unit that allows me to control the water temperature remotely, if I choose to do so.

Installing a Spa Shower

WEEKEND AT THE SPA OUT OF THE QUESTION? HOW ABOUT A HOME SPA — IN AN HOUR.

There's nothing wrong with a nice hot shower. But when you want to make it something special, you can replace the old standby here with a spa.

1 This is our guest bathroom, and I'd been thinking it would be nice to do something special for our guests when they visit. I decided replacing the standard shower head with a hydro-massage, spa-type head. Perfect!

2 They say it only takes a few minutes to put this in ... and I'm gonna try it out.

3 First I need to remove the existing shower head. It just unscrews from the shower arm, though you may need an adjustable wrench to get it started. Once loose, the head will unscrew easily by hand.

4 To remove the arm, I insert the arm of my multi-groove pliers into the end, and give it a twist. By the way, this is a great way to tighten a shower arm, too — without damaging the finish.

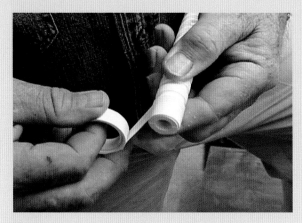

5 This threaded plastic pipe nipple will replace the shower arm I just took out. Two or three wraps of Teflon tape will make sure the threads tighten properly to prevent leaking.

6 An adjustable wrench snugs the nipple in place.

7 To leave the required amount of nipple exposed, I cut away the excess with a hack saw as directed by the instructions.

8 This is a combination shower head and diverter. It screws directly onto the shortened plastic nipple, leaving the nipple completely concealed.

9 That's all it takes to install the shower head and diverter. Now I'm going to start on the vertical spa unit by first drawing a plumb (perfectly vertical) line down from the center of the shower head.

10 I place the vertical spa on top of the line and mark the locations for the top and bottom mounting screws.

11 A hammer drill with a carbide-tipped masonry bit makes short work of drilling into the grout line.

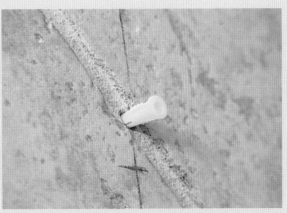

12 I insert a plastic anchor into the top hole, and tap it into place with a hammer.

13 The bottom hole must be drilled through the face of the tile, so I use a spring-loaded center punch to make a small dimple in the tile face that will prevent the masonry bit from skating ...

14 ... and make sure the hole ends up exactly where I want it. I then tap another plastic anchor into this hole.

15 Next, I attach the vertical spa with screws at the top and bottom.

16 End caps slip into place to hide the hardware ...

17 ... and I then attach the water supply hose to the inlet on the shower head.

18 Counting the time it took me to read the directions (and I did read them, in this case) I put this up in a little less than an hour. I have to say, this is a nice, luxurious addition to this bathroom.

19 A comforting standard shower for every day ...

20 ... and a vertical spa arm for a massaging affect. And the nozzles are adjustable to accommodate both short and tall people.

Fixing a Damaged Hose

THIS IS A QUICK FIX THAT WILL SAVE YOU SOME MONEY

Our local home improvement center employee shows us how to fix a damaged hose. It takes about five minutes and you're ready to start the water flowing again.

1 Look familiar? This is what happens when the car meets the hose. Don't worry, you don't have to buy a whole new hose. You can fix it, and it's not very expensive at all. Let me show you how.

2 First, you have to remove the bad end. A sharp pair of scissors will do the job.

3 You have a few choices when it comes to fittings. Some are made of plastic and are the least expensive.

4 It clamps on. You insert the hose, tighten the screws, and voila, you're good to go!

5 Brass fittings will last longer. This one comes with a hose clamp. Same principle as the plastic — the hose inserts into the fitting, you clamp it down and you're good to go. My only issue here is that the hose clamp can be cumbersome.

6 My personal favorite is this brass model. There's a sleeve that slides over the cut end of the hose ...

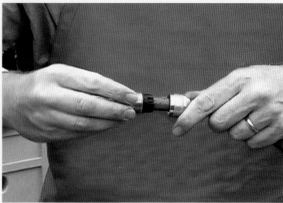

7 ... then you insert the fitting onto the end ...

8 ... slide the sleeve up to the fitting ...

9 ... align the threads ...

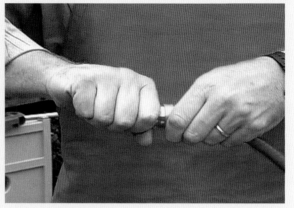

10 ... and screw it in place ...

11 ... and you're back in business

Automatic Irrigation System

**GIVE YOUR PLANTS THE WATER THAT THEY NEED
TO GROW, EVEN WHEN YOU'RE NOT HOME**

You know the longer I live in my home, the more I enjoy my gardening. But I've got one problem when it comes to watering. I'm on the road a lot and sometimes several days can go by and my plants don't get any water.

1 I've got several different situations.

2 Container plants ...

3 ... foundation plants ...

4 ... and flowering plants. So what I'm going to do is install an automatic drip irrigation system. It will water the plants even if I'm not home and take into account their individual requirements.

5   As much as two-thirds of the water we use in our homes is actually used taking care of our yard and plants. A drip irrigation can save up to seventy percent over other watering methods. My drip irrigation system is going to start right here with this hose bib or faucet.

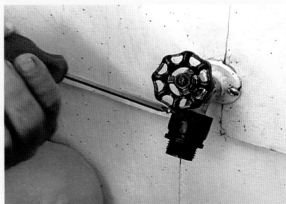

6   First I screw on this check valve. It's designed to keep the irrigation water from flowing inside the house and contaminating my household water supply. Tightening this set screw will keep vibration (or kids) from loosening the valve.

7   Next I'll turn this single faucet into four, using what's called a hose bib manifold.

8   These are pressure reducers. In a lot of homes, water pressure can run sixty to eighty pounds per square inch. This is too much pressure for a drip irrigation system. So this device drops it down from household pressure to something in the twenty to twenty-five pound range.

9 In the area that I'm irrigating, there are several different kinds of plants with different water requirements. So I've set up three zones. Each one will be served by one of these outlets. This fourth one over here will be for my garden hose.

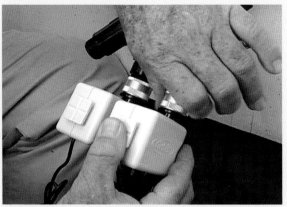

10 I want the water to come on and turn off automatically. So the next step is to install (just screw on) an automatic valve. These electronic valves operate using low voltage electricity.

11 They'll turn the water on or off for each zone when they're instructed to do so. This is the brain of my automatic drip irrigation system. It's a timer or controller, is completely weather proof and battery operated.

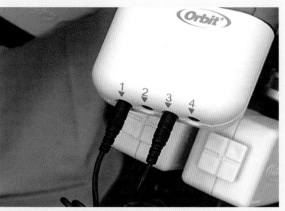

12 The electronic valves simply plug into the controller like this.

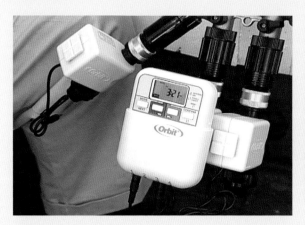

13 The controller mounts on the front of one of the valves. All I need to do is program it to tell each automatic valve which day of the week and time of the day to come on and how long to run.

14 Now I need to set up a distribution system to get the water from the valves to the plants. I'll do that using this half-inch polyethylene tubing. A couple of tips: One; invest in a pair of these cutters.

15 And two; put the tubing out in the sun a couple of hours before you start. That will warm it up and make it more pliable. With one end cut, I connect it to the automatic valves.

16 Since I have fairly deep mulch on my bed, I'm going to lay the tubing on top of the ground. So all I have to do is rake a shallow trench.

17 Then, use tubing stakes to anchor the run in place. When I reach the end of a run of tubing, I have to close or cap it off.

18 There are a couple of ways to do this. One is to take a figure-eight clip like this, slip it over the tubing, bend the tubing and then slide the clip back up to keep the tubing bent. Sort of like bending a garden hose to stop the flow of water.

19 Another way to end a run of tubing is with a cap like this. When winter weather comes, I can just unscrew the cover and drain the lines while the half inch polyethylene tubing brings water into the general area.

20 This smaller quarter inch tubing delivers it to individual plants or groups of plants.

21 To attach the smaller tubing to the longer, I first use a special punch to make a small hole.

22 Then snap in a connector ...

23 ... slip on a piece of quarter inch tubing and cut it to length.

24 On the ends of the tubing go the emitters — small nozzles, if you will — that emit anywhere from one to four gallons of water per hour in a variety of patterns.

25 Drip emitters like this are extremely efficient. Delivering water directly to the base of the plant.

26 Misters, sprayers and sprinklers are often mounted on higher stakes and distribute water in quarter circle, half circle, full circle, and rectangular patterns. Just one of these can water several plants at the same time.

27 For my container plants, I'm going to use something called soaker tubing. The water penetrates through the wall of the tubing.

28 It's very easy to use. I start by putting a "T" in the end of the quarter inch tubing like this.

29 Next I place one end of the soaker tubing onto one arm of the "T", lay the soaker tube around the base of the plant, cut it to length and slip the end of the tube on the other arm of the "T".

30 With this part of my irrigation system in place and ready to go to work, I can rake the mulch back over the tubing ...

31 ... making it invisible, yet accessible. The tubing can also be buried more deeply if desired.

32 A trench just a few inches deep is adequate. First make an angle cut through the turf using a flat garden spade. Then lever the sod upward to create a shallow groove. Set the tubing in the bottom of the cut, then press the grass back into place.

33 This is called a sidewalk tunneling tool. It's simply a plastic nozzle attached to a length of PVC pipe, with a hose connected to the opposite end.

34 The stream of water bores a hole in the dirt under the sidewalk.

35 Once I'm through, I use PVC pipe cutters to snip off the nozzle and the connector.

36 The plastic pipe stays in place and acts as a conduit. I just push the irrigation tubing through it. A couple of connections and my irrigation is complete. It's good to know that even if I'm on the road, my plants won't suffer because of it.

Creating a Waterfall

BRING SOME WATER TO THE DESERT.

Today I'm in Sedona, Arizona which is surrounded by enormous red-rock formations, some of which are said to be vortexes — energy centers that some people believe bring harmony and balance to one's life. Perhaps that's what attracted Doreen and Paul Sloven, who retired here a couple of years ago.

1 Doreen and Paul love spending time outdoors and it's no wonder. They have a spectacular view. They would like to add a waterfall in their front yard, built up from natural stone. I'm going to help them do just that.

2 Our first step is to define the perimeter of the pond using a stick to trace the outline in the dirt.

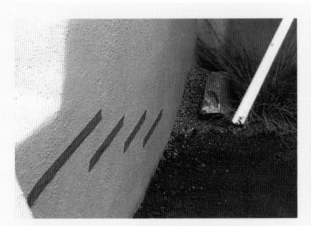

3 Then we'll plan the contours and height of the stone wall, which will be stacked right in front of the existing wall. Tape works best to experiment with various heights.

4 With the outline drawn in the dirt, I follow the line with some chalk powder to get a better visual idea of how this is going to look. If something isn't right I can just cover it over and redraw it. It's important to lock in the design now before digging.

169

5 We grab some shovels and start digging out the entire area outlined by the chalk.

6 We're going to dig about one-and-a-half to two feet deep.

7 While Paul finishes the digging, I begin compacting the soil with a tamper.

8 This is a pond liner. It's heavy gauge puncture-resistant vinyl. We're going to line this entire hole and part of the wall with this.

9 We temporarily tape one edge of the liner up on the wall behind what will eventually be a rock waterfall.

10 The liner prevents water from leaking out of the pond and will keep the existing wall from getting wet. While I finish taping it to the back wall, Doreen and Paul tuck it into the hole.

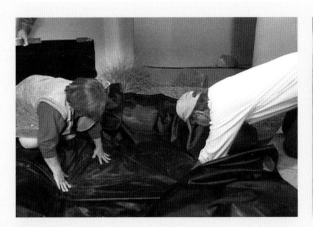

11 We want the liner to fit like a glove. A snug fit will make it less visible when the pond is full of water. We'll cut away the excess later on with a pair of scissors.

12 Now we're ready to begin stacking the stone wall. Paul and Doreen have ordered the stones and have laid them out on the front yard so that we can get a good look at each one.

13 We're going to have to select these individually, one-by-one, to build up the wall for the waterfall.

14 Here's number one.

15 Picking the rocks is a little bit like piecing together a puzzle. You look for stones with similar width and thickness and edges that will fit well together.

16 Because these rocks are not perfectly flat we sometimes need to use a shim to level them. The shims are just thin pieces of rock that we insert under a stone to raise it up.

17 Before the wall gets too much higher, Doreen runs a hose behind the stones to what will eventually be the top of the waterfall. A pump in the bottom of the pond will push the water up the hose and out the top where it will flow down the face of the rock.

18 We've kept the wall level from left-to-right but put a slight tilt from back-to-front to let the water run off the front edge of these rocks and eventually into the pond. We've also staggered the joints whenever possible to make the wall look better and make it stronger.

19 Once we finish the back wall, Doreen and Paul arrange stones around the edge of the pond ...

20 ... making sure they overhang slightly to conceal the liner.

21 Meanwhile, I hook up the pump and we place it at the deep end of the pond. The pump will be plugged into an outdoor receptacle. In addition to circulating the water, it will also filter it — especially important since Paul and Doreen plan to add fish someday.

22 Next we cover the bottom with clean round stones that will help conceal the liner ...

23 ... then fill the pond with water ...

24 ... and plug in the pump.

25 The pump works fine, but this single stream of water shooting out of the wall is not exactly what we're looking for.

26 So, I make up a water manifold from plastic pipe that will better distribute the water ...

27 ... allowing it to cascade gently over the face of the rocks.

28 After all that rock hauling I'd say it's Advil time. But in the course of a day we've created a desert oasis that sounds every bit as beautiful and relaxing as it looks.

Ponds and Fountains with Pre-Formed Liners

TAKE THE PLUNGE AND SEE IF A POND OR FOUNTAIN COULD BE A NICE ADDITION TO YOUR YARD

This beautiful old Victorian has been home for the past five years to David and Suzanne Holmes and their children, Katie and Robbie. The view from their second story balcony is dominated by the side wall of their garage — a perfect location for a backyard refuge.

1 These pre-cast plastic pond liners are going to form the basis of our fountain. David and Suzanne love the sound of cascading water.

2 This style of pre-formed liner is designed for just that purpose. The water comes in at the top and then it flows off into the pool.

3 There are smaller versions too, that we can stack to emphasize the waterfall effect.

4 We try a few different sizes of the pond liners, and when we're happy with our selections, Suzanne outlines the bottom liner with chalk.

5 We then move the liner out of the way ...

6 ... and start digging. Since most of the pond liner will remain above ground to give us more height for our waterfall, we only remove about three inches of soil.

7 I ask Dave and Suzanne to dig away a few inches along the garage for a precautionary step. Because we're up against a wood-frame building, I want to build a concrete block wall between the fountain and garage to prevent any water seepage to the garage. Suzanne tamps the soil ...

8 ... and Dave follows behind with a bag of leveling sand.

9 I set the first block in place a couple inches out from the wall.

10 Wiggling the blocks in the sand helps us level each one. Getting the first course right is critical to making the entire wall level and stable.

11 Before laying our second course, Suzanne applies a bead of landscape-block adhesive.

12 This, along with the fact that we're spanning the joints with each new course, will give the wall its structural integrity.

13 With the wall complete, Robbie and Katie give their parents a breather and help me spread some sand where the liner will rest.

14 A flat and level surface is what we're after here.

15 We bring the liner back into the space and work the liner into the sand.

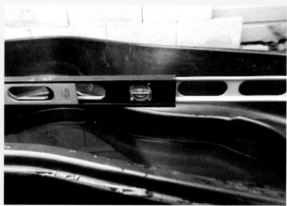

16 Then we do a rough check for level, start adding water, and continue to check for level as the liner settles into the sand.

17 After a final check, we pack sand into any voids around the base of the liner.

18 Now we're going to build a decorative retaining wall around the outside of the pond with these blocks. We start by placing a dozen or so around the liner.

19 I've taken away the stones we laid out and replaced them with these small green flags to mark the outside of our wall.

20 But we also have to make sure that this wall is level. That's the reason for the level line. The ground rises up about two inches here, which means we're going to have to dig a little bit of dirt away down there.

21 We remove the sod and dig out a bit of soil.

22 Then we begin setting our stones back in place, adjusting them so that the tops are level with the string.

23 After the first course is in, we again apply more of our landscape-block adhesive to the top ...

24 ... and begin setting our second course in place. The lips on the bottoms of the blocks allow them to interlock with each other as they're stacked.

25 When we met the next morning (yes, I would recommend this as a two-day project), we admired our work for a moment and then got back to work.

26 Our first job today is backfilling the area between the wall and the pond line with gravel, which will help with drainage.

27 Next we cover the gravel with a few inches of sand, stopping at the top of the second block.

28 We fill up the remaining space between the wall and liner with bark mulch.

29 This row of stones above the liner is going to serve two purposes. It will begin to hide the side of the our next highest liner and it's going to give us a ledge upon which to rest the top-pond liner on. I think one more block should do it.

30 Now we fill the area back with some more mulch.

31 Water will always flow downhill, but you can never be absolutely sure what path it will follow, so while we don't have any of our pond liners in permanent position, it's a good time to add some water and see if we need to adjust any of the upper pools.

32 Looks like we were right on the money.

33 The mechanics of our pond here are pretty simple actually. It consists of a pump and a filter. There are two hoses coming out of the filter that go to the upper ponds.

34 I'm going to submerge the pump and filter into the water. It's designed for underwater use. The wiring and mechanics are sealed against moisture, protecting from electrical shock.

35 While I let the pump fill with water, Dave and Suzanne conceal the hoses by snaking them through the rocks to the upper ponds.

36 The outlet is protected by a ground fault circuit interrupter, or GFCI, and is housed in a weatherproof box, into which the pump is plugged.

37 With water flowing, we're down to our final steps ...

38 ... adding plants, including floating water lilies ....

39 ... some decorative floating glass balls and, of course, some fish.

40 To provide some height to the setting we're using a metal trellis upon which we hang flowering baskets.

41 Our cascading pond has brought not only additional beauty, but also the calming sound of a babbling brook to the backyard.

42 If Suzanne and David ever grow tired of it, they can easily redesign their pond to suit their changing tastes.

Creating a Backyard Fish Pond

HAVE YOUR OWN STOCKED FISH POND, WATER PLANTS AND ROCKS TO SIT ON

During a recent trip through Minnesota, I had the chance to view some amazing outdoor ponds. So I've decided I've got to have one for myself. I've been looking around the yard and I think I've found the perfect spot near a wild cherry tree.

1 Chick Kelty is Mr. Pond, and he and his crew have agreed to give me a hand. He likes the location I have in mind and suggests laying out the shape, using a garden hose.

2 Next, I use spray paint to mark the profile.

3 Then I start cutting through the sod around the rim with an edger.

4 After scoring the side, Chick and I remove the sod one piece at a time. With it gone I can see the shape.

5 This is the main pond filter. We position it near the edge of the pond and mark the location.

6 The waterfall filter will go on the opposite side of the pond.

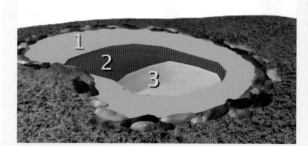

7 The pond will be divided into three levels. Providing natural ledges on which to place rocks and gravel that will conceal the pond liner.

8 Chick and I start digging. This part of the country has a whole lot of stone walls — and for good reason. The ground around here is full of rocks. We encounter our fair share. Finally though, we reach the bottom.

9 This pond underlayment will act as a protective cushion and will help prevent any rocks or roots from damaging the pond liner which is the next thing to go into the hole.

10 Chick and I lay it in place ...

11 ... fold it where needed and smooth out some of the wrinkles.

12 Rob Dieter is a water garden specialist. You could say he's a rock artist. And he's got a real knack for placing these hunks of stone in just the right places.

13 When he's finished, they'll look so convincing you'd think Mother Nature had a hand in it.

14 While Rob's rocking away, we drop the main filter in the hole we dug and start backfilling around it.

15 With most of the big stones in place, it's time to fill in the gaps and cover the ledges with gravel.

16 When we're finished, the rocks and gravel will completely disguise the rubber liner. This piece of stone, weighing nearly five hundred pounds, is going to have a special place in the pond. I'm calling it my fishin' and gazin' rock.

17 A bit more gravel brushed in the right places, this fiberglass wannabe rock to cover the main filter and a few stones to camouflage the edge of the liner.

18 Finally we wash the rock while pumping out the muddy water.

19 A backyard water feature like this one is often referred to as a living pond. Mine will include a half dozen different aquatic plants ...

20 ... moss near the waterfall and of course, fish.

21 Brightly colored koi!

22 We'll keep them in the bag for now and let them gradually acclimate to the pond water.

23 As an accent, Rob recommends I pick up a few flat river rocks that we'll lay on top of the gravel to add a bit more texture.

24 Plants will make a pleasant transition zone between the pond and the lawn.

25 You know, I've always wanted waterfront property.

26 What I learned from those folks in Minnesota ...

27 ... is, I don't have to move to the water ...

28 ... I can bring the water here.

Other Plumbing

Install a Central Vacuum

OUT OF SIGHT, QUIET AND POWERFUL.

Until recently, I'd never thought much about having a central vacuum system. But once I began considering the advantages -noise reduction, convenience and cleaner air, I started warming up to the idea and finally decided to put one in.

1 Well, actually, I guess it might have been the stairs that convinced my wife Lynn and I of the merits of a central vac.

2 Carrying the canister vacuum up and down between floors was bad enough.

3 But when you're sweeping the steps ...

4 ... and the vacuum heads for the first floor without you, it's time to rethink things.

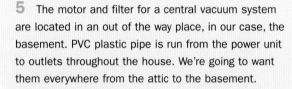

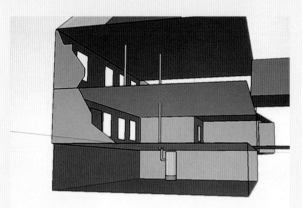

5 The motor and filter for a central vacuum system are located in an out of the way place, in our case, the basement. PVC plastic pipe is run from the power unit to outlets throughout the house. We're going to want them everywhere from the attic to the basement.

6 For this project I've teamed up with Chris Ellis, an installer for Cyclone Home Systems. I really hope to do this project without opening up the walls. Frequently they look for closets to run the piping, but the closets I was considering don't line up for all the floors.

7 But I do have a laundry chute that goes up to the second floor. Chris agrees this is our best bet.

8 The laundry chute will allow us to run pipe from the basement clear up to the attic without having to open a wall. Good news!

9 Chris collects his tools and a bundle of plastic pipe ...

10 ... and we begin by drilling a hole through the bottom of the laundry chute ...

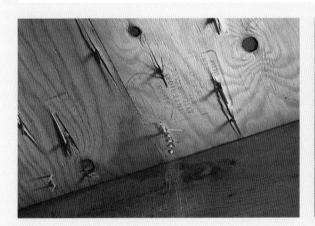

11 ... and into the basement.

12 With our pilot hole drilled, Chris widens the hole to accommodate the PVC piping with a hole saw.

13 With the hole in the first floor, giving us access to the basement, we turn our attention to the attic. First, Chris and I cut out a portion of the attic floor in search of the top of the chute.

14 After pulling out some insulation, I'm pretty sure we have indeed found the top of the laundry chute. To make sure, Chris heads back down to the second floor.

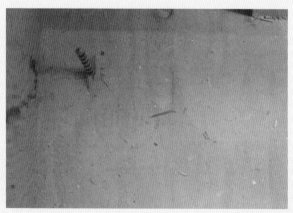

15 Drilling up through the top panel of the laundry chute should give us our answer.

16 And sure enough, the bit pops out close to where we'd expected.

17 Another minute with the hole saw ...

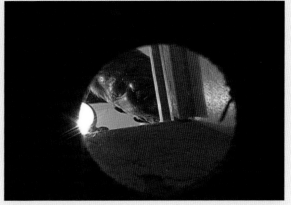

18 ... and we're through.

19 To make sure the holes are aligned, I drop a plumb bob all the way from the attic into the basement.

20 Now we have a way to get the PVC pipe from the power unit up to the attic. From the attic, the plan is to run the pipe downward inside the walls to reach the outlets on the second floor. Well, we're almost through the top plate when ...

21 ... Murphy is at work again. We've drilled into a veritable minefield of nails and screws.

22 So we're left with no choice but to move over and try again.

23 With a clean hole at the top, Chris goes down to the second floor and pushes a screwdriver through the wall where we plan to locate the outlet.

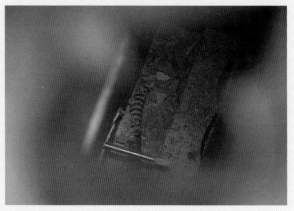

24 I check the alignment from above, and it looks good.

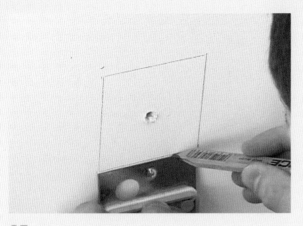

25 So Chris marks ...

26 ... and cuts out the opening for the outlet.

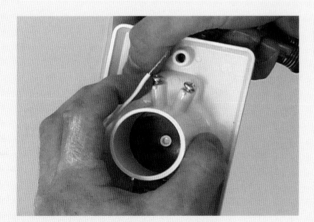

27 A low voltage wire will run through the wall and all the way back to the power unit. When the hose is plugged in, the wire will carry a signal that turns on the vacuum.

28 Chris connects an elbow to the back plate ...

29 ... inserts the plate into the wall ...

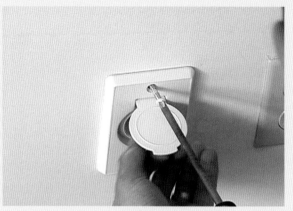

30 ... then attaches the cover with a couple of screws.

31 Next is the fixture for the wall of the master bedroom. We're accessing it by adding an "L" to that outlet, like I have here, but the pipe is running up through the attic and then down again all the way into the basement.

32 So this is the pipe coming up out of the bedroom, crosses over here. Now we're ready to go all the way down to the basement

33 Next we'll run the pipe across the attic. We cut the PVC pipe to length and attach it to the fittings.

34 The joints are welded with PVC adhesive and whenever possible, the pieces are assembled outside of tight quarters ...

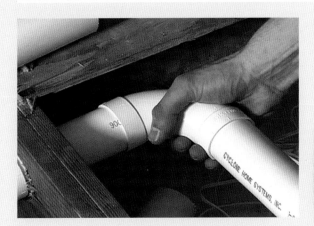

35 ... and then set into place in section.

36 To install the first floor outlets, Chris drills holes from the basement up inside the walls, cuts an opening, installs the low voltage wire and outlet fixture, attaches the cover plate, then feeds the PVC pipe up from below to make the connection.

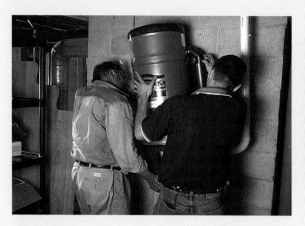

37 We've installed a total of six outlets. One in the attic, two on the second floor, two on the first floor and one in the basement. And all the pipe leads to one place, the central vacuum power unit, that simply hangs on the wall.

38 All that's left for us to do is connect the piping to the central power unit ...

39 ... plug it in and flip the switch.

40 Chris points out the built-in muffler system on the side of the canister to even further reduce the noise produced by the vacuum motor.

41 All of our outlets have been located near electrical receptacles so that we can easily plug in the cord for the power head.

42 I won't say a central vacuum will turn housework into play but a system like this can deliver a lot of suction very quietly ...

43 ... and make navigating around a house like this, a heck of a lot easier.

Install a Portrait Fireplace

**FIREPLACE AMBIENCE AT EYE LEVEL IN
JUST ABOUT ANY ROOM.**

I love fireplaces and I'm fortunate
to have two here in the house ...

1 But one place I've always wanted a fireplace but never had one, is right here in the kitchen. Why the kitchen? Because like most families, we spend a lot of time hanging out here. I'd like to do is bring the ambience of the family room fireplace into the kitchen.

2 To get some ideas, I go online and start a search, and discover a fireplace concept that's new to me — something called a *portrait* fireplace. Portrait fireplaces are usually up off the floor, closer to picture height. They're also smaller.

3 Small enough, in fact, to fit snugly into a corner like this one in the kitchen. The fireplace that I've chosen comes with its own cabinet, and the installation is straightforward enough. But because it involves a gas line, electrical and venting, you should be fairly comfortable with your skills for this project.

4 The first step is removing the baseboards in the corner where the fireplace will sit. First, cutting through the caulk with a sharp utility knife. This will avoid tearing the wallboard when the base is pulled off.

5 Next, a prybar is used between the baseboard and wall. We slip in a wide putty knife behind, to keep from denting or crushing the wallboard.

6 Then we start working on the natural gas supply. First, an exploratory hole is drilled through the floor.

7 We check in the basement to make sure our hole will clear pipes and wiring.

8 Once we're satisfied there are no obstructions, we drill two larger holes through the floor. One for a shutoff valve and the other for a gas line.

9   Next, the base cabinet is carried in and set in place.

10   We drill an inch-and-a-half hole through the top ...

11   ... and then he gas line is then pushed through the floor ...

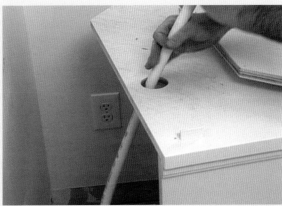

12   ... and pulled up through the hole in the cabinet.

13 An electronic stud sensor is used to locate wall studs near the corner.

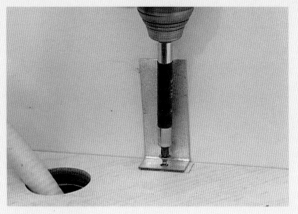

14 Then, metal brackets are mounted to the cabinet deck ...

15 ... and attached to the studs with screws.

16 With the cabinet base secure, the core of the fireplace, the firebox and burner, is set temporarily in place ...

17 ... and the vent location marked on the interior wall.

18 Then the firebox is removed and the vent collar is held in position and the shape is traced on the wall.

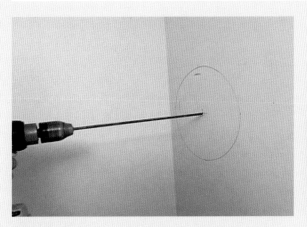

19 A long bit is used to bore a locator hole through the center, to the outside wall.

20 Then the wallboard is cut away at the inside.

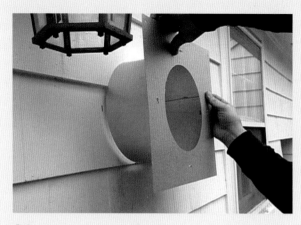

21 On the outside, the exterior portion of the vent is centered over the locator hole. The vent outline is traced on the wall ...

22 ... and the exterior shingles and sheathing are cut away, using a reciprocating saw.

23 The vent collars are checked for alignment and set into position.

24 Next, the vent cap is set in place ...

25 ... the outline is traced ...

26 ... and the shingles are cut away, using a circular saw. The blade depth is set so that it cuts only through the shingles, and not into the sheathing.

27 The cut shingles around the opening are removed.

28 Then, the vent collar is slipped in place ...

29 ... and the vent cap eased into position ...

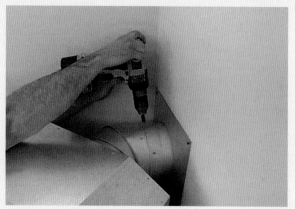

30 ... the vent sections screwed together ...

31 ... and the cap is attached to the sheathing.

32 Finally, silicone caulk is applied around the edge of the vent cap.

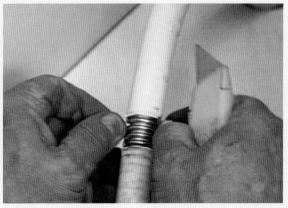

33 Now we can connect the natural gas line to the burner. First, we install a brass connector to the unit.

34 Next, insulation is stripped away from the outside of the flexible gas line ...

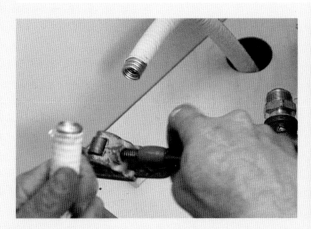

35 ... and the line is cut line to the correct length.

36 A nut is slipped over the end of the gas line ...

37 ... a split ring is added ...

38 ... a nut is slipped over the split ring ...

39 ... and the line is attached to the brass fitting on the burner. Everything is then tightened using a pair of wrenches.

40 In many areas, ours included, code requires an easily accessible shutoff valve within three feet of a gas appliance.

41 This flush-mounted valve on the floor can be turned on and off with a key. With the gas connection complete, it's time for a safety check.

42 The plumber who is lending me a hand turns on the gas at the valve and uses this portable detector to test the line, fittings and connections. The instrument will sense even minute gas leaks in a matter of seconds.

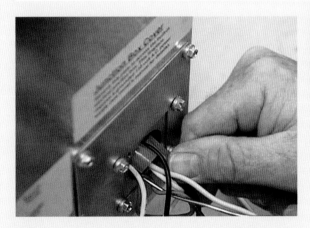

43 Because the fireplace has a built-in fan, it requires an electrical connection. Wires are twisted together, secured with wire nuts — and tucked carefully inside the junction box.

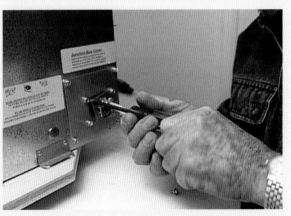

44 The box cover is attached in place ...

45 ... and the strain relief screws tightened.

46 What we have now is a functioning heater, capable of putting out over 16,000 BTUs. But in the next few steps, this is going to go from just a heater to a portrait fireplace.

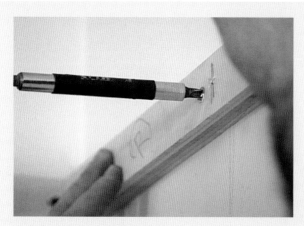

47 Next, wooden cleats are attached to the wall on both sides of the corner.

48 Then it's time to bring in the upper cabinet, and set it in place, surrounding the burner and firebox.

49 Screws are run through the top and into the wall cleats, securing the upper section to the wall.

50 Now the tempered glass face plate is removed ...

51 ... and a ceramic fiber liner installed. The liner not only acts as a heat shield between the firebox and cabinet, it also reflects heat outward.

52 The burner is disguised with a ceramic plate that looks like a charred wood remnant.

53 Next, the ceramic logs are set in place. These lock in specific positions to look convincingly like partially burned firewood. But what happens next is responsible for giving the fireplace an even more realistic look.

54 These coal-like nuggets are also made of ceramic and, along with this fibrous version of the material, some of which is shredded and applied by flaking it off with a stiff brush, will radiate a warm red color that bears a striking resemblance to glowing embers.

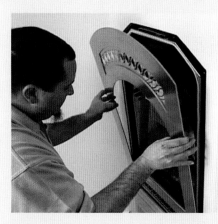

55 With everything ready, the tempered glass plate is put back and covered with a decorative face which is available in a variety of metals and finishes.

56 Well, I got my kitchen fireplace: Everything I wanted, and more.

57 Ambience, a great source of heat and well, I won't be carrying wood for this one, because I've got remote control.

58 Maybe there's room for another portrait fireplace in the bedroom ...

Relocating a Clothes Washer

WASHING MACHINE NOT IN THE MOST CONVENIENT LOCATION? MOVE IT.

Our laundry room, like many, is just about big enough for the washer and dryer. When I think about it though, a lot happens in that space besides washing and drying. There is sorting, folding, ironing … why, it's a beehive of activity. Maybe that is why my wife, Lynn, wants to make every square inch count, and that meant moving the washer and dryer.

1 Well I've come up with a reorganizing plan that I think is going to work quite well. It involves moving this, the washer and dryer, from over here...

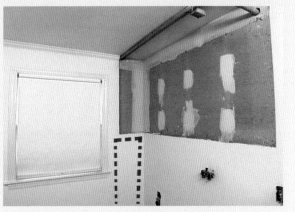

2 ... to this wall underneath the window.

3 I begin by installing a recessed shutoff valve and outlet box.

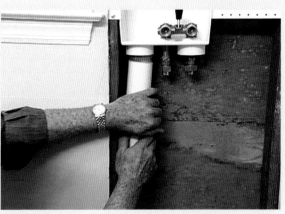

4 Once it's in place, I start putting together the drainpipe.

OTHER PLUMBING

5 The drain will pass through the floor and into the basement below, where I'll hook it up to the existing system.

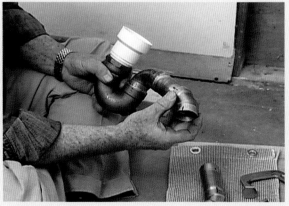

6 When putting together pipe runs with lots of twists and turns, I pre-assemble sub-sections ...

7 ... then solder the remaining joints, once everything's in place.

8 When I'm soldering against an interior (and potentially flammable) wall, I use a fire proof cloth behind the pipes.

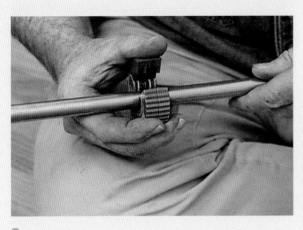

9 Next, I cut smaller, half-inch copper pipe for the water lines ...

10 ... and attach then to the shutoff valve.

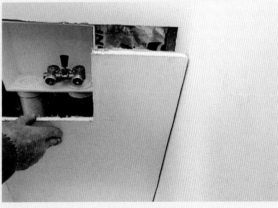

11 Because this is an exterior wall, I'm using foam insulation sleeves and also packing plenty of fiberglass between the pipes and the outer wall.

12 The last step here is to replace the wallboard.

13 Both the washer and dryer will need electrical outlets. After cutting the holes, I thread wire up from the basement ...

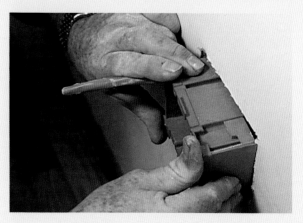

14 ... set the boxes in place ...

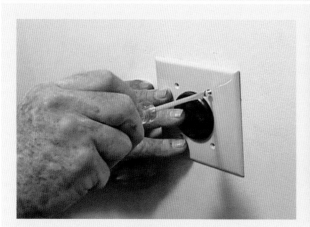

15 ... connect the receptacles and attach the cover plates.

16 I'm locating the hole for the dryer vent so that it's directly opposite the outlet on the machine. I start with a small pilot hole made with a long bit.

17 I drill all the way through the wall and out through the siding on the outside. This pilot hole will ensure a straight hole for the vent.

18 Next I use a hole saw, large enough to accommodate the vent pipe, to complete the hole. A pilot bit on the hole saw fits into my pilot hole I drilled earlier.

19 Once I'm through the wallboard, I move to the outside to drill through the siding and complete the hole, again, using my pilot hole to guide the hole saw.

20 With the hole bored, I slide the vent pipe, with attached flange, into place.

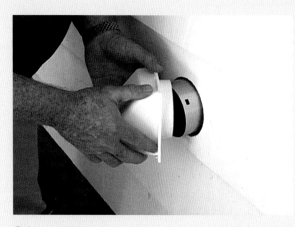

21 A vent cover is slipped over the vent pipe on the outside and screwed in place.

22 Back inside, I hook up my water supply lines.

23 Hot-to-hot and cold-to-cold, or I'll have some trouble with all that sorted laundry ...

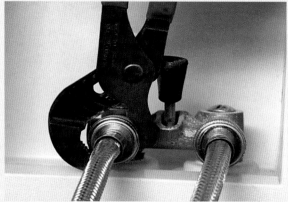

24 ... and finally tighten the supply fittings with adjustable pliers.

25 My drain hose drops into place in the drain access and I'm ready to test out my work.

26 The new location works great for gaining extra space in this small room. And the washer is working fine. Wonder if I can get someone else to test the ironing board?

Definitions

Aerator – A device screwed into the end of a faucet spout that mixes air into flowing water, and controls flow to reduce splashing. It sometimes contains a baffle to reduce flow to 2.5 gpm.

Angle Seat Wrench – Valve seat wrench with a handle that includes a 90- degree bend.

Aquifer – A layer or zone below the surface of the earth which is capable of yielding a significant volume of water. The upper level of the aquifer is called the water table.

Auto Pilot – A gas pilot device which automatically shuts off the gas supply to the appliance burner if the pilot flame is extinguished.

Back Flow – The circumstance of water traveling from one system back into any part of the main distribution system, usually by siphoning.

Ball Check Valve – A valve that uses a ball to seal against a seat to stop flow in one direction.

Ballcock – The fill valve that controls the flow of water from the water supply line into a gravity-operated toilet tank. It is controlled by a float mechanism that floats in the tank water. When the toilet is flushed, the float drops and opens the ballcock, releasing water into the tank and/or bowl. As the water in the tank is restored, the float rises and shuts off the ballcock when the tank is full.

Basin Wrench – A wrench with a long handle with jaws mounted on a swivel that allows the jaws to reach and handle nuts to fasten faucets to a previously installed sink.

Black Water – Wastewater from toilets or latrines and sinks used for food preparation or disposal, or for the disposal of chemicals.

Bleed – To drain a pipe of excess air by opening a valve at the end of the pipe.

Bonnet – The top portion of a compression valve assembly, it holds the valve in place as it is tightened against the valve seat at the other end of the assembly.

Butterfly Valve – A valve made of a square, rectangular, or round disk attached to a shaft inside a body of the same shape. Rotating the shaft 90 degrees opens or closes the valve.

Cleanout Plug – A plug in a trap or drain pipe that provides access for the purpose of clearing an obstruction.

Drain – Any pipe that carries wastewater or water-borne waste.

Elbow – A fitting with two openings that changes the direction of the line. Also known as an ell. It comes in various angles from 22½ degrees to 90 degrees; often referred to by their angles (i.e. 45, 90).

Element – Heating unit in an electric water heater.

Female Fitting – A fitting that receives a pipe or fitting. A fitting into which another fitting is inserted.

Fixture – A device that provides a supply of water or its disposal, e.g. sinks, tubs, toilets.

Flapper Valve – The part on the bottom of the toilet tank that opens to allow water to flow from the tank into the bowl.

Flexible Connector – A braided hose that connects a faucet or toilet to the water supply stop valve. Serves as a riser but is much more flexible and easier to install. Usually stainless steel or PVC/Polyester reinforced hose.

Float Ball – The floating ball connected to the ballcock inside the tank that rises or falls with changing water levels in the tank, and actuates or shuts off the ballcock as needed.

Flue – A passageway for combustion by-products.

Flush Ball – Flapper.

Flush Valve – Flapper Valve.

Flux – Paste applied to copper pipes and fittings before soldering to help the fusion process and prevent oxidation.

Gray Water – Waste water from sinks, showers, and bathtubs, but not toilets.

Hanger – A device used to support pipes.

Male Fitting – Fitting that is inserted into another fitting.

Mixing Valve – Mixes hot and cold water to achieve a specified delivery temperature.

Nipple – A short length of pipe installed between couplings or other fittings.

Nonpotable – Not suitable for drinking.

Overflow Tube – The vertical tube inside a toilet tank that directs water into the bowl in case the ballcock malfunctions. It is usually part of the flush valve. It prevents potential water damage caused by a tank overflow. A "constant-running" condition alerts the user to a problem. On most toilets, the overflow tube also has a refill tube flowing into it, which directs water from the ballcock through the overflow tube to the bowl, after a siphon break.

Packing – Fibrous material that is used on faucets to prevent leaks.

Packing Nut – Nut that holds the stem of a faucet in position & holds the packing material.

Petcock – A small faucet for draining liquids or relieving air pressure.

Potable – Water suitable for drinking.

Refill Tube – The tube that directs water from a ballcock into the overflow tube to refill the bowl after a siphon break.

Shutoff Valve – Most commonly refers to angle stops installed under sinks and toilets, but also valves installed on branch lines and alongside the meter.

Solder – A metal alloy that is melted to create a fused joint between metal pieces. Also the act of melting solder into the joint.

Stem – Part of the faucet that holds the handle on one end and the washer on the other.

Sweating – Slang term for soldering. Also formation of condensation on the outside of pipes or toilet tanks.

Tee – T-shaped fitting with three openings that allow another pipe to be joined at a 90 degree angle, used to create branch lines.

Teflon Tape – A fluorocarbon polymer with non-sticking properties used to wrap pipe threads to seal a joint.

Trap – Curved section of drain line that prevents sewer odors from escaping into the atmosphere. All fixtures that have drains must have a "P" trap installed. A toilet is the only plumbing fixture with an "S" trap.

Vent Stack – Upper portion of the soil stack above the topmost fixture through which gases and odors escape.

Suppliers

ADAMS & KENNEDY — THE WOOD SOURCE
6178 Mitch Owen Rd.
P.O. Box 700
Manotick, ON
Canada K4M 1A6
613-822-6800
www.wood-source.com
Wood supply

ADJUSTABLE CLAMP COMPANY
404 N. Armour St.
Chicago, IL 60622
312-666-0640
www.adjustableclamp.com
Clamps and woodworking tools

B&Q
Portswood House
1 Hampshire Corporate Park
Chandlers Ford
Eastleigh
Hampshire, England SO53 3YX
0845 609 6688
www.diy.com
*Woodworking tools, supplies
and hardware*

BUSY BEE TOOLS
130 Great Gulf Dr.
Concord, ON
Canada L4K 5W1
1-800-461-2879
www.busybeetools.com
Woodworking tools and supplies

**CONSTANTINE'S WOOD CENTER
OF FLORIDA**
1040 E. Oakland Park Blvd.
Fort Lauderdale, FL 33334
800-443-9667
www.constantines.com
Tools, woods, veneers, hardware

FRANK PAXTON LUMBER COMPANY
5701 W. 66th St.
Chicago, IL 60638
800-323-2203
www.paxtonwood.com
Wood, hardware, tools, books

THE HOME DEPOT
2455 Paces Ferry Rd. NW
Atlanta, GA 30339
800-430-3376 (U.S.)
800-628-0525 (Canada)
www.homedepot.com
*Woodworking tools, supplies
and hardware*

KLINGSPOR ABRASIVES INC.
2555 Tate Blvd. SE
Hickory, N.C. 28602
800-645-5555
www.klingspor.com
Sandpaper of all kinds

LEE VALLEY TOOLS LTD.
P.O. Box 1780
Ogdensburg, NY 13669-6780
800-871-8158 (U.S.)
800-267-8767 (Canada)
www.leevalley.com
Woodworking tools and hardware

LOWE'S COMPANIES, INC.
P.O. Box 1111
North Wilkesboro, NC 28656
800-445-6937
www.lowes.com
*Woodworking tools, supplies
and hardware*

MICROPLANE
2401 E. 16th St.
Russellville, AR 72802
800-555-2767
www.us.microplane.com/
*Rotary shaper and other
wood-shaping tools*

ROCKLER WOODWORKING AND HARDWARE
4365 Willow Dr.
Medina, MN 55340
800-279-4441
www.rockler.com
Woodworking tools, hardware and books

TOOL TREND LTD.
140 Snow Blvd. Unit 1
Concord, ON
Canada L4K 4C1
416-663-8665
Woodworking tools and hardware

TREND MACHINERY & CUTTING TOOLS LTD.
Odhams Trading Estate
St. Albans Rd.
Watford
Hertfordshire, U.K.
WD24 7TR
01923 224657
www.trendmachinery.co.uk
Woodworking tools and hardware

VAUGHAN & BUSHNELL MFG. CO.
P. O. Box 390
Hebron, IL 60034
815-648-2446
www.vaughanmfg.com
Hammers and other tools

WATERLOX COATINGS
908 Meech Ave.
Cleveland, OH 44105
800-321-0377
www.waterlox.com
Finishing supplies

WOODCRAFT SUPPLY LLC
1177 Rosemar Rd.
P.O. Box 1686
Parkersburg, WV 26102
800-535-4482
www.woodcraft.com
Woodworking hardware

WOODWORKER'S HARDWARE
P.O. Box 180
Sauk Rapids, MN 56379-0180
800-383-0130
www.wwhardware.com
Woodworking hardware

WOODWORKER'S SUPPLY
1108 N. Glenn Rd.
Casper, WY 82601
800-645-9292
http://woodworker.com
Woodworking tools and accessories,
finishing supplies, books and plans

Index

More great titles from Popular Woodworking and Betterway books!

THE COMPLETE GUIDE TO CONTRACTING YOUR OWN HOME

By Dave McGuerty & Kent Lester

This step-by-step guide to managing the construction of your own home is jamb packed with:

- To-do check lists for each phase of the construction process
- Hundreds of illustrations that clearly show what the author is teaching you
- Pages and pages of each necessary form you'll need to complete your home project

ISBN 13: 978-1-55870-465-7
ISBN 10: 1-55870-465-5
paperback, 320 p., #70378

ISBN 13: 978-1-55870-817-4
ISBN 10: 1-55870-817-0
paperback, 160 p., #Z1027

THE SMART WOMAN'S GUIDE TO HOMEBUILDING

By Dori Howard

Using the information in this book, you can:

- Improve your communication with homebuilding professionals
- Make informed decisions to keep you on schedule
- Get insider advice from experts in homebuilding
- Stay on budget and on time!

POPULAR WOODWORKING'S ARTS & CRAFTS FURNITURE PROJECTS

This book offers a collection of twenty-five Arts & Crafts furniture projects for every room in your home. Some projects are accurate reproductions while others are loving adaptations of the style.

A bonus CD-ROM contains ten projects and ten technique articles to provide even more information on construction and finishing.

ISBN 13: 978-1-55870-846-4
ISBN 10: 1-55870-846-4
paperback, 128 p., #Z2115

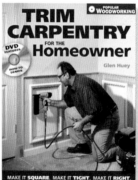

ISBN 13: 978-1-55870-814-3
ISBN 10: 1-55870-814-6
paperback with DVD, 128 p., #Z0953

TRIM CARPENTRY FOR THE HOMEOWNER

By Glen Huey

Master carpenter Glen Huey shows you:

- How to use ready-made supplies and materials from home center stores
- How to install or replace door, window, chair moulding and other room trims
- How to make and trim out fireplace surrounds and mantles
- How to install wainscotting and built-in furniture

These and other great woodworking books are available at your local bookstore, woodworking stores, or from online suppliers.

www.popularwoodworking.com